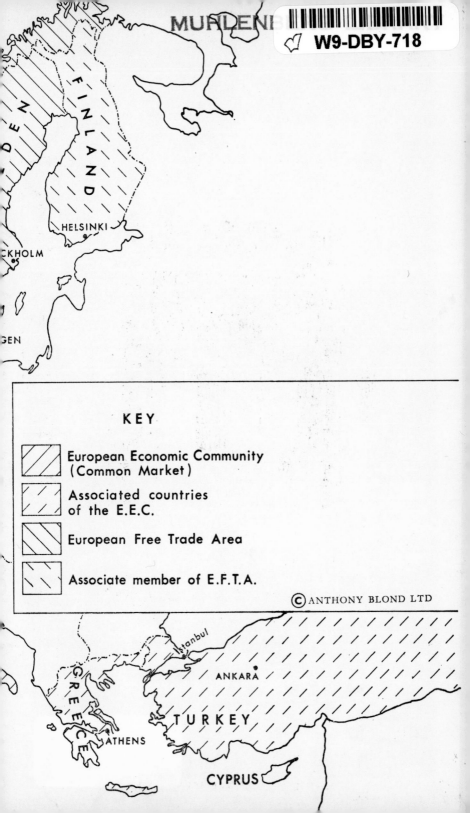

MURLENE

W9-DBY-718

FINLAND

HELSINKI

CKHOLM

DEN

GEN

KEY

European Economic Community
(Common Market)

Associated countries
of the E.E.C.

European Free Trade Area

Associate member of E.F.T.A.

İstanbul

GREECE

ANKARA

TURKEY

ATHENS

CYPRUS

Published in the United States
by **DUFOUR EDITIONS, INC.**
Chester Springs, Pa. 19425

THE COMMON MARKET

The Great Society

Other titles in the series:

The Common Market

the Treaty of Rome explained

Edited by John Calmann

ANTHONY BLOND

*First published in 1967
by Anthony Blond Ltd.,
56 Doughty Street,
London WC1*

Reprinted 1967

© Anthony Blond Ltd. 1967

Printed in Great Britain by W. & G. Baird Ltd., Belfast

Contents

Preface

MEMBERSHIP of the Common Market, which is based on the Treaty of Rome, is today a major aim of British foreign policy. Nevertheless many people are still unclear about what the Rome Treaty says and how the European Community works, although the Community's advantages and disadvantages have been widely discussed in the press and on television and radio. This book sets out to answer these questions.

The first chapter, on the Treaty itself, analyses, article by article, what the six original members set out to achieve through it, and the methods of economic integration which they chose. Each of the Treaty's sections has a heading of its own, and progress so far on each part is briefly described. The second chapter on the structure of the Community describes the working of the institutions of the Common Market, those of its precursor, the European Coal and Steel Community, and those of the European Atomic Community. It describes how the policies on which the Councils of Ministers drawn from the Six member countries have agreed are prepared and implemented. The third chapter outlines in some detail the achievements of the Community and measures the extent of integration in the various economic sectors covered by the Treaty. The fourth chapter, on political union, clarifies the main concepts on which the European Community is based, and shows how they lead, in theory, to a further stage in relations between member states which goes beyond economic union.

The book ends with a brief analysis of the British quest for membership, and outlines the main problems which the British government is facing in the present pre-negotiation period.

All the chapters except the first are drawn from *Western Europe: A Handbook* (Anthony Blond, 1967). Given the special importance which the Common Market has for Britain today, it was felt that a separate issue of these chapters would be particularly useful.

J.C.

THE TREATY OF ROME

DEREK PRAG

The Treaty of Rome setting up the European Economic Community (EEC or Common Market), signed on the Capitoline Hill in the heart of the ancient city on 25 March 1957,[1] is both an international treaty and a written constitution. Under its terms six Western European nations—Belgium, France, the Federal Republic of Germany, Italy, Luxembourg and the Netherlands—already linked since 1951 in the European Coal and Steel Community (ECSC), voluntarily delegated certain of their sovereign national powers to common or Community institutions. These powers were surrendered peacefully, without coercion or pressure, in order that they might be exercised jointly and for the general gain. The objective was full economic union—a giant stride along the road to 'an ever closer union' of the European peoples.

Under the ECSC Treaty signed in 1951, known as the Treaty of Paris, many powers were delegated directly to the ECSC executive body, the High Authority; they were, however, limited to the industrial sectors of coal, steel and iron ore. Under the Rome Treaty, which covered the whole of the six nations' economies, and therefore involved a much wider transfer of powers, the major powers of decision were delegated, by and large, not to the executive body, the EEC Commission, which represents the general Community interest, but to the Community body on which the national interests are represented—the Council of Ministers.[2]

The Rome Treaty also differs from the Paris Treaty in its fundamental structure: the Rome Treaty is a 'framework' treaty, setting out a series of objectives and deadlines by which these objectives must be reached—an outline which is gradually to be filled in by the Economic Community itself through the formulation of detailed policies and the issue of regulations. The common agricultural policy is a typical example: the Treaty sets out the general aims of this policy and lays down that common rules and Community-wide organisation of the market will be in force by the end of the transition period; the details of the policy were completed only in 1966 after years of tough bargaining between the Six, and will be implemented by a large number of detailed regulations. The Paris Treaty, on the other hand, is a complete set of basic rules and regulations for 'governing' the coal, steel and iron-ore industries of the Community.

[1] A second treaty was signed at Rome on the same date setting up the European Atomic Community (Euratom) aimed at pooling the nuclear research of the six member countries. The treaty setting up the EEC, commonly known as 'the Treaty of Rome', is the one with which this chapter is concerned. For Euratom see 'The Structure of the European Community'.

[2] See 'The Structure of the European Community', p. 32.

9

Despite these fundamental differences, the Rome and Paris Treaties are both forms of written constitution—sets of basic law for the institutions they set up. The idea of pooling sovereignty and of vesting it in Community bodies by means of written constitutions at first aroused mistrust and distaste both in Britain and in other European countries. It is, however, the foundation stone of the Communities, and unless one remembers this it is impossible to understand many of the courses which have been taken.

A further point essential to the understanding of the Rome Treaty follows naturally from this voluntary pooling of certain sovereign powers and from the Treaty's role as the constitution for an economic union of the Six. This is the complex balance the Treaty strikes, first between the interests of its member countries, and secondly between its institutional, or constitutional, components. Superior advantage to the French in agriculture balances superior advantage to the Germans in industry, or to the Benelux countries in commerce and the transit trade; for Italy, special measures were envisaged, in the shape of the European Investment Bank, the Social Fund and provisions for a common policy on occupational training, to deal with its particular regional problems of underdevelopment and chronic unemployment. Institutionally, the complex interaction of the Council of Ministers and the Commission in the decision-making process, together with the possibility of majority voting in the Council, provides the means of avoiding deadlock, resolving disputes, safeguarding national interests, in particular the interests of the smaller countries and at the same time, through the action of the Commission, keeping the general Community interest firmly in view.

If sometimes the Rome Treaty seems to be regarded with a reverence foreign to 'pragmatic' peoples outside the Community, it is not because of any tendency towards mysticism on the part of those who defend it. It is because the Treaty and its implementing regulations form the whole legal basis for the Community's existence; destroy or distort a part of it, and one or other of the member countries' interests are affected, the constitutional balance is disturbed, and the signal may be given for the gradual undermining of the whole edifice and its promise of future achievement.

The Preamble and the Principles (Articles 1–8)

The preamble of the Rome Treaty clearly summarises the basic philosophy behind the Treaty and the Common Market's role as the foundation 'of an even closer union among the European peoples'. The Treaty sets out, through the establishment of a Common Market and the gradual alignment of economic policies, to further harmonious economic development throughout the Community, continuous, balanced expansion, and faster growth in living and working standards (Article 2). The Community is to achieve this by: abolishing customs duties, quantitative restrictions, and other trade barriers; establishing a common tariff for imports from all non-member countries; abolishing obstacles to free movement of people, services and capital; adopting common policies for agriculture, transport and foreign trade, and for competition; coordinating economic policies; harmonising national legislation; setting up a Social Fund and a European Investment Bank; associating the overseas territories and ex-territories of member states so as to increase their trade and aid their economic and social development (Articles 3 and 6).

The member states pledge themselves to carry out all the obligations arising from the Treaty or from the acts of the Community institutions (listed in Article 4), to aid the latter in accomplishing their mission, and to refrain from any measures likely to jeopardise the attainment of the Treaty's objectives (Article 5). All discrimination on the basis of nationality is banned and the Community can take any measures necessary to apply this ban (Article 7).

For the task of establishing the Common Market, the Treaty envisaged a transition period of 12 years, divided into three stages of four years (Article 8). Although the first and second stages could have been prolonged, none of the member states requested this and the Community passed automatically into the second stage at the beginning of 1962 and into the third stage at the beginning of 1966.[1] The third stage, due to end on 31 December 1969, can still be prolonged, but only by unanimous decision of the Council of Ministers voting on a proposal of the Commission, and in any case the total prolongation of the transition period cannot exceed three years. With these possible exceptions, the Common Market (customs union and economic union) must be complete by the end of the transition period and all the policies and rules envisaged by the Treaty must be in force by then. In practice, the customs union (abolition of all internal tariffs and other trade barriers, and application of the common external tariff) will be complete by 1 July 1968, and on the same date all the main provisions of the common agricultural policy, which were finally decided in the summer of 1966, will also be in force.

The Foundations of the EEC

Free movement of goods

The Community is based on a customs union covering trade in all goods. This means the banning of all customs duties (and charges with equivalent effect) on imports and exports between the member states—not only of goods made in the Community countries but also those imported from outside— and the adoption of a common external tariff (Article 9). Goods imported from non-member countries are considered free to circulate (*en libre pratique*) if customs duties and other requisite charges have been levied on them in one of the member states (Article 10).

The Customs Union

The abolition of internal customs duties. The Rome Treaty blocked the imposition of all new import and export duties and charges of equivalent effect in trade between member countries (Article 12) and (Articles 13–15) set out rules and a timetable on which the Commission based its directives for gradually abolishing all import duties between member states over the transition period. The level of duties on which the reductions were made was that in force on 1 January 1957 (Article 14).

In practice the Community has been able to move faster than the Rome Treaty envisaged (this is specifically permitted by Article 15); by 1 January 1966 internal customs duties had been reduced by 80 per cent, and in July 1966 the Council of Ministers agreed that the remaining 20 per cent would be removed by 1 July 1968—18 months ahead of schedule.

Export duties and charges of equivalent effect were abolished by the end of the first stage. Duties levied for revenue purposes have also to be abolished

[1] See 'Customs Union and Economic Union in the EEC', p. 44.

but the Treaty allows them to be replaced, if the member state concerned wishes, by internal taxes (Article 17).

The common external tariff. As later in the Treaty in the section on foreign trade, the Six open the section on the common external tariff by declaring their willingness to help in the development of international trade and the reduction of trade barriers on a basis of reciprocity (Article 18). In general, the duty levels for each item of the common tariff were calculated as the arithmetical average levels of the six national tariffs at 1 January 1957, with the exception of items enumerated in lists B (raw materials), C, D (raw materials and semi-manufactures) and E (certain chemicals) annexed to the Treaty, for which the duty levels could not exceed 3, 10, 15 and 25 per cent respectively; for lists F (food, some other agricultural products and some raw materials) and G (certain 'sensitive' products), tariff levels were negotiated between the member states (Articles 19 and 20).

When the common external tariff is fully in operation, it will give the Community the lowest tariff of any of the world's major industrial nations or groupings. Eighty per cent of all Community duties lie between 4 and 19 per cent, and the Community's average tariffs are considerably lower than those of either Britain or the United States for every major industrial sector. Overall, the Community's tariff averages 11·7 per cent compared with 18·4 per cent for Britain and 17·8 per cent for the United States.

By its decision of July 1966 the Council agreed that the common external tariff would enter fully into force on 1 July 1968, replacing entirely the national tariffs for goods coming from outside the Community. This move, which follows two alignments (on 31 December 1961 and 1 July 1963) each reducing by 30 per cent the gap between the national tariff levels and those of the common tariff, will take place 18 months ahead of the timetable originally laid down in the Treaty (Articles 22 and 23). All tariffs for which the difference between the national duty levels and the common tariff levels was less than 15 per cent were replaced by the common tariff level on 31 December 1961.

For a wide range of products (mainly raw materials and semi-manufactures), member states may be granted tariff quotas at a reduced or nil rate of duty, and for some products member states may be authorised to suspend or partly suspend their duties (Article 25). Modifications or suspensions of common external tariff duty rates require the unanimous approval of the Council, but temporary changes of up to 20 per cent of the duty rate can be effected by qualified majority from 1970 onwards (Article 28).

By the end of the first stage, the member states were to have harmonised—'to the extent necessary'—their legislative and administrative practices in customs matters (Article 27) but this task had not been completed by the scheduled date nor indeed by the end of 1966. The Commission hoped to complete this task as part of 'Operation 1 July 1968' to ensure that by that date there will be complete freedom for movement of goods within the Community.

Quantitative restrictions and state monopolies

The Rome Treaty banned quantitative restrictions and measures with equivalent effect between member states (Article 30) and set out a complex timetable for enlarging existing quotas until by the end of the transition period they no longer constituted any restriction on trade (Articles 32–5). In fact, all quantitative restrictions on industrial goods between member states were abolished by the end of the first stage of the transition period

(December 1961). However, restrictions can still be applied by member states for reasons of public morality, order and safety, for protection of the life and health of persons, animals and plant-life, and for protecting national artistic and historical treasures and industrial and commercial property (Article 36). The Commission considers it essential to unify these measures in order to avoid discrimination and disguised restrictions.

Finally, the Treaty provides in Article 37 for the adaptation of state monopolies so as to remove by the end of the transition period all discrimination between nationals of member states in supply and marketing. This article, which covers all bodies through which a member state controls or influences imports or exports between member states, should have been applied at the same pace as quantitative restrictions were removed on the products in question. Although the French and Italian tobacco monopolies have already substantially liberalised their import policies, a good deal still remains to be done to end discrimination and restriction, both for tobacco and for other state monopolies (e.g. petroleum, potash, alcohol) in some Community countries.

Agriculture

With the common market in agriculture now entering into force and the common agricultural policy decided for all the major products, the long section of the Rome Treaty on agriculture (Articles 38–47), which sets out principles, procedures and transitional arrangements, is mainly of academic interest only. Article 38 includes agriculture and trade in farm products in the Common Market and provides for the establishment of a common agricultural policy. The aims of this policy (Article 39) are: to raise productivity and efficiency in farming; to provide the farming population with equitable living standards, notably by raising income levels; to stabilise markets; to guarantee security of supply; to ensure reasonable prices for consumers. The Treaty permits the use of all measures necessary to reach these objectives, including price regulation, production and marketing subsidies, stockpiling and carry-over systems, and common import and export stabilisation schemes.

The common agricultural policy which has been developed (it was to all intents and purposes completed by decisions taken in May and July 1966) is based on three main features: common marketing policies; a common policy for external trade, replacing the previous national systems of protection for most product groups by a single Community system of variable import levies and minimum import prices, while exports are subsidised by a system of 'refunds'; and finally a common policy to raise productivity and efficiency in farming. Common policies for all the major product groups (grains, beef and veal, pigmeat, poultry, eggs, fruit and vegetables, sugar, fats and oils, and rice) were to be in force by 1 July 1967. Meanwhile, the Commission still had to present proposals for tobacco, fish, hops and non-edible horticultural products.

The basis of the common market for agriculture has been the setting of common price levels. These come into force for the various products between November 1966 and 1 July 1968, and will enable 90 per cent of all farm produce to be traded freely without restriction throughout the Community from 1 July 1968 onwards.

From July 1967 the whole cost of financing the common agricultural policy ($1,400–$1,500 million a year) will be financed centrally by the Community through the European Agricultural Guidance and Guarantee

Fund. The Fund's resources will come from levies on imports, which will cover 45 per cent of total expenditure, and, until the end of 1969 at any rate, from government contributions covering the remainder.[1]

Free movement of persons, services and capital

Workers

By the end of the transition period workers must be able to move freely to take up offers of jobs anywhere in the Community, stay in any of the member states in order to work there, and live in a member state after having worked there; these provisions do not, however, cover posts in public administration (Article 48). Free movement of workers is to be achieved through close cooperation between national authorities, by bringing together offers of work and people seeking employment, and by gradually abolishing administrative procedures and practices—especially waiting periods—and all other restrictions which hinder the free movement of workers or impose on workers from other member states conditions different from those applied to national workers in the choice of employment (Article 49). The member states undertake to promote a joint programme for exchange of young workers (Article 50) and to take all necessary steps to ensure that all social security contributions, in whatever member state they may be paid, count for benefit eligibility, and that benefits are payable anywhere in the Community (Article 51).

Most of this programme had been carried out by the end of 1966, but a third regulation was still required to make freedom of movement complete.

The right of establishment

Nationals of any of the member states—whether individuals or companies (Article 58)—must by the end of the transition period be freed from all restrictions on setting up in another member state, or on establishing agencies or branches (Article 52). The right of establishment includes the right to exercise non-wage-earning activities (e.g. professions) and to constitute and run companies under the same conditions as nationals of the member state (Article 52).

In October 1961 the Community published a detailed programme for the removal of restrictions on the right of establishment in all the different branches of activity and the stages by which they were to be reached (Article 54). It gave priority to sectors in which freedom of establishment would be particularly beneficial to the development of production and trade; the programme will permit workers employed in a member state other than their own to stay in that country in order to take up a non-wage-earning activity, allow the purchase and use of real estate in a member state other than that of the person or firm concerned, and abolish all restrictions on staff from a parent firm entering a branch or agency set up in another member state (Article 54). The same article provides for coordination of company law as far as necessary to achieve the right of establishment.

Activities involving the exercise of public authority in a member state are excluded from the provisions on the right of establishment, and other exceptions can be made (Article 55). As in the case of various other Rome Treaty provisions, discrimination against nationals of other member states is permitted, exceptionally, for reasons of public order and safety and public health, but the laws and regulations governing such discrimination must be coordinated (Article 56).

[1] See also below under *The Community Institutions: Financing the Community*.

To facilitate access to and exercise of professions, steps are being taken to ensure reciprocal recognition of degrees, diplomas, certificates and other qualifications (Article 57). The Treaty lays down that this extremely complex and difficult task should be completed by the end of the transition period, but work on it was considerably behind schedule at the end of 1966.

Services

Parallel with the removal of restrictions on the right of establishment—i.e. the right to set up in a member state other than that of which a person or firm is a national—the Treaty also provides for the removal of restrictions on supplying services (notably those of an industrial or commercial nature, arts and crafts, and the exercise of the liberal professions) in member states other than that in which the supplier of the service is established (Article 59). The supplier of services must be allowed temporarily, as well as permanently if he so wishes, to exercise his activities in the country where the service is supplied on the same terms as nationals of that country (Article 60).

In October 1961, at the same time as it published its programme for the right of establishment, the Community also published a detailed timetable for the removal of restrictions on the supply of services, giving priority to services which directly affect production costs or whose freeing furthers trade in goods (Article 63). As long as such restrictions remain in force, they must be applied without distinction of nationality or residence (Article 65). Articles 55-8 (see above) also apply to the removal of restrictions on supplying services.

Capital

The member states undertook to abolish by the end of the transition period, and to the extent necessary for the efficient operation of the common market, restrictions on movements of capital held by residents of the six countries, and to abolish all discrimination based on nationality, residence or the place in which the capital is held (Article 67). Current payments in connection with capital movements are freed. National rules and regulations governing the capital and money markets must, when applied to freed capital movements, be exercised without discrimination (Article 68).

The Commission must also submit to the Council proposals for gradual coordination of the six countries' exchange policies concerning capital movements between the Six and non-member countries. (Should these steps fail to eliminate divergences, with the result that the freeing of capital movements was used to evade the exchange-control rules of one of the member states *vis-à-vis* non-member countries, that state could take appropriate steps after consulting the other member states and the Commission— Article 70). Member states must keep the Commission informed of capital movements to and from non-member countries (Article 72).

Should capital movements disturb the capital market of a member state, governments may take defensive measures, subject to authorisation by the Commission; such authorisation can be revoked by the Council. An emergency procedure covers cases where secrecy or urgency is essential (Article 73).

The two directives on capital movements already issued (in May 1960 and December 1962) removed, conditionally or unconditionally, almost all restrictions arising from exchange control, but left some connected with short-term money movements. However, national legislative provisions and administrative practice still impose a wide enough variety of controls to prevent the creation of a large capital market. A third directive, which would have abolished discriminations by one member state against nationals of other member states in the issuing and placing of shares and the acquisition of shares by financial institutions, was submitted to the Council by the Commission in April 1964, and a directive to replace taxes on capital issues, placings, transfers, etc. by a single Community 'contribution tax', was submitted in December of that year, but neither had been adopted by the end of 1966. The Commission is convinced that country-by-country arrangements are inadequate in this field, and that the Community economy requires a European capital market geared to its needs.

Transport

The Rome Treaty envisages a common transport policy (Article 74), to be adopted by the end of the transition period and based on common rules applicable to international transport starting or ending in the territory of a member state or passing through one or more member states (Article 75). Aids are permitted for the coordination of transport or the maintenance of a public service (Article 76). Despite the submission of a whole series of proposals by the Commission, no major decisions were taken on the common transport policy until June 1965, when the Council adopted the general principles on the basis of which implementing regulations were to be worked out in two stages—one by the end of 1969 and the other by the end of 1972;[1] no implementing regulations had been adopted by the end of 1966.

The Treaty also bans all discriminations involving the application of different rates and conditions for similar goods and hauls by reason of the country of origin or destination of the goods carried (Article 79). Rules to suppress discrimination came into force in July 1961; they require transport rates and conditions to be notified to the Commission and are backed by powers for the Commission to inspect books and impose fines.

Member states are forbidden to apply prices and conditions comprising any element of support or protection, for one or several enterprises or industries, to transport hauls inside the Community. However, in examining prices and conditions the Commission must take account of the needs of regional policy and underdeveloped regions, and of the effects on competition between different forms of transport. Moreover, the ban does not cover rates fixed for reasons of competition (Article 80). Charges for crossing frontiers must not exceed a reasonable level related to the real costs involved and an effort must be made to reduce these costs (Article 81). A transport committee of experts appointed by the governments assists the Commission (Article 83).

The Treaty provisions on transport apply to rail, road and inland waterway transport. The Council decides by unanimous vote whether, to what extent and by what means any measures should be taken for sea and air transport (Article 84); so far no steps have been taken by the Council in this direction.

COMMUNITY POLICY

Common rules

The rules of competition

Rules applying to enterprises. The Treaty bans and renders null and void agreements, decisions to associate, and concerted practices which have as their aim or effect to prevent, restrain or distort competition, and in parti-

[1] See 'Customs Union and Economic Union in the EEC', p. 49.

cular price-fixing, restriction of production, sales outlets or investments, market-sharing, price discrimination and conditional sales, if they are likely to affect trade between member states. However, the ban can be waived on certain conditions for arrangements which contribute to better production or distribution, or promote technical or economic progress (Article 85). Article 86 imposes a similar ban on the abuse of dominant positions in the market by one or several enterprises.

A regulation detailing the measures for implementing these bans was adopted in December 1961.[1] It has been followed by a series of supplementary regulations and decisions which, through the precedents they create, are gradually setting a pattern and establishing a body of anti-trust case-law for the Community.

The member states themselves, in respect of publicly owned enterprises and enterprises benefiting from exclusive or special rights, are subject to the Treaty rules of competition (Article 90).

Dumping. If, during the transition period, following a request by a member state or other interested party, the Commission confirms that dumping is being practised in the Common Market, it addresses recommendations to those responsible for it, with a view to bringing it to an end. If the practices continue, the Commission may authorise the member state affected to take counteraction. Dumped products may be sent back, without payment of import duty or other restriction, to the member state they came from (Article 91).

State aids (subsidies). State aids in general, of whatever kind, are forbidden in so far as they affect trade between member states, if they distort or threaten to distort competition by favouring certain enterprises or productions. However, social aids to individual consumers and aids to deal with natural or other calamities are permitted; aid for the economic development of regions suffering from unemployment or with low living standards, for important projects of Community interest, or for remedying serious economic dislocation in a member state, may be permitted; any other form of aid may be specially authorised by unanimous vote of the Council (Article 92).

The Commission is bound by the Treaty to keep state aids under continuous scrutiny and to propose measures necessary for the development and operation of the Common Market. If it decides that aids are incompatible with the Common Market under Article 92, or are applied abusively, it must ask the member state concerned to abolish or modify them. Governments must inform the Commission of any plan to institute or modify state aids, and cannot implement their intentions until a decision has been taken (Article 93).

Draft regulations for implementing the Treaty provisions on state aids were submitted to the Council by the Commission in 1966 but at the end of the year the bulk of the work of classifying the different state aids into the three categories of compatible, incompatible and possibly compatible with the Common Market still remained to be done, with agricultural aids a particularly important problem.

Fiscal matters

A member state may not impose, directly or indirectly, internal taxes of any kind on products of the other member states at a level higher than that which it imposes on similar national products; nor may it impose on them taxes which indirectly protect other products. Any taxes that did not conform to

[1] See 'Customs Union and Economic Union in the EEC', p. 48.

this provision were due to be abolished by the end of 1965 (Article 95) and some action has been taken. The amounts refunded on goods exported to other member states must not exceed the internal charges actually levied on them (Article 96).

Member states which levy turnover tax on the cumulative multi-stage (*cascade*) system may, for the internal taxes which they levy on imported goods or for refunds on exported goods, fix average rates by product or product group as long as these do not infringe Articles 95 and 96 (Article 97). For charges other than turnover taxes, excise duties and other indirect taxes, exemptions and refunds cannot be granted on exports to other member states, and compensatory taxes on imports cannot be imposed, without prior approval by the Council, and then only for a limited period (Article 98).

Article 99 requires the Commission to propose to the Council ways of harmonising member states' legislation on turnover taxes, excise duties and other indirect taxes, including compensatory charges on trade between member states. The Commission in November 1962 presented proposals for harmonising first the systems and then the rates of turnover tax, on the basis of the French added-value system; the Council adopted regulations introducing a Community turnover tax based on the added-value system in February 1967.

Reducing the gap between legal provisions

Steps must be taken to reduce the gaps between those legislative and administrative provisions of member states which have a direct incidence on the operation of the Common Market (Article 100). Where the Commission finds that a disparity between the legislative and administrative provisions of member states distorts the conditions of competition in the Common Market, it attempts to promote an agreement between member states for eliminating the distortion; if agreement cannot be reached directives may be issued by qualified majority (Article 101). When there is reason to fear that introduction or modification of a legislative or administrative provision may cause distortion, the member state concerned must, before carrying out its plans, consult the Commission, which recommends steps to avoid the distortion (Article 102).

The Community has already adopted regulations covering a wide range of subjects, notably for foodstuffs, where national legislation on such matters as permissible dyestuffs and preservatives constituted an important trade barrier, and for pharmaceutical products.

Economic policy

Short-term economic policy (*politique de conjoncture*)

Member states consider their short-term economic policy as a matter of common interest and the Council can take appropriate measures for any situation.[1] The need for a common short-term economic policy appeared less pressing in 1966, with an almost automatic balance achieved between differing economic trends in member states. But the Commission believed that full integration, in which all barriers are removed and the economy advances in step throughout the Community, would mean that inflationary or deflationary movements spread rapidly to the whole of the economy. The Commission therefore hoped to work out with the Council in 1967 a rapid, effective procedure which would enable the Council to take immediate action on Commission proposals.

[1] For a summary of the many steps taken in this field see 'Customs Union and Economic Union in the EEC', pp. 49–51.

Balance of payments

Each member state undertakes to pursue the economic policy necessary to ensure equilibrium in its overall balance of payments and to maintain confidence in its currency, while taking care to ensure a high level of employment and price stability (Article 104). With this aim in view, member states undertake to coordinate their economic policies, and to institute for this purpose cooperation between their administrations and central banks. These links have already been forged, notably in the form of the Central Bank Governors' Committee set up in April 1964. A Monetary Committee, two members of which are appointed by each of the member states and two by the Commission, has been set up to help coordinate member states' monetary policies; its task is to report regularly to and draw up opinions for the Council and the Commission on the monetary and financial situation of the member states and the Community (Article 105).

Each member state undertakes to authorise, in the currency of the member state where the creditor or beneficiary resides, payments relating to movement of goods, services or capital, and also transfers of capital and wages, in so far as movement of goods, services and capital has been freed between the member states (Article 106).

Each member state must treat its exchange-rate policy as a matter of common interest; if it devalues or revalues its currency in a manner which is not in conformity with Article 104 and which seriously distorts the conditions of competition, the Commission can authorise the other member states to take steps, strictly limited in duration, to counter the consequences of this action (Article 107).

Where a member state experiences balance-of-payments difficulties likely to jeopardise the operation of the Common Market or the establishment of the common commercial policy, the Commission immediately examines its situation and the action it has taken and recommends measures. If the action taken by a member state and the measures suggested by the Commission appear insufficient to overcome the difficulties, the Commission recommends to the Council the application of mutual-aid provisions. These may take the form of joint action in other international organisations, steps to avoid trade diversion if the country in difficulties maintains or reimposes quantitative restrictions with regard to non-member countries, and the granting of limited credits by the other member states. Moreover, during the transition period, mutual aid may also take the form of special tariff cuts or quota enlargements aimed at encouraging an increase in imports from the country in difficulties. Finally, if the mutual aid recommended by the Commission has not been granted by the Council, or if it is granted but proves insufficient, the Commission can authorise the state in difficulties to take safeguard measures which it prescribes. The Council may revoke or modify such authorisation (Article 108). In case of a sudden balance-of-payments crisis where mutual aid is not immediately granted, the member state concerned can take the necessary safeguard measures without prior authorisation (Article 109).

Commercial (foreign-trade) policy

The Treaty envisages (Articles 111 and 113–16) a common commercial policy to be applied from the end of the transition period onwards. It involves:

—The undertaking of all tariff negotiations by the Commission on behalf of the Community, on the basis of a mandate and directives from the

Council of Ministers, and in consultation with a special committee (known as the 111 Committee); this provision is applicable from the start of the transition period (Article 111);

—the conduct of commercial policy on uniform principles, notably for tariff changes, the conclusion of tariff and trade agreements, the alignment of liberalisation measures, export policy, and also measures for trade protection, including those against dumping and subsidies; as with tariff negotiations, the Commission negotiates on behalf of the Community on the basis of a mandate and directives from the Council (Article 113);

—cooperation by the member states should trade diversions threaten to hold up the carrying out of the common commercial policy, or if the latter causes economic difficulties in one or several member states (Article 115);

—joint action only, for all matters of particular interest for the Common Market, in international economic organisations (Article 116).

During the transition period member states undertake to coordinate their trade relations with other countries (Article 111), to harmonise their aid systems for exports to other countries (Article 112), and to consult each other with a view to concerted action, and as far as possible a uniform position, in international economic organisations (Article 116).

Member states declare that in establishing a customs union they intend to contribute to the harmonious development of world trade and the gradual removal of barriers to international exchanges (Article 110). The common commercial policy must take into account the favourable effect which the abolition of internal customs duties may have on the competitive power of firms in the member states.

In accordance with Article 111, all tariff negotiations in the General Agreement on Tariffs and Trade (GATT), both in the Dillon Round and in the Kennedy Round, have been conducted by the Commission on behalf of the Community; the Commission has also conducted the negotiations for the trade agreements which were concluded with Iran (1963), Israel (1964) and the Lebanon (1965).

In the other fields, however, a great deal still remains to be done if a common commercial policy is to be in force by the end of the transition period. There is still no unified Community position in bodies such as the United Nations Conference on Trade and Development (UNCTAD); Community lists of liberalised imports need to be drawn up, not only for goods from GATT countries but also for those from Eastern Europe. Moreover, with the free circulation of imported goods rapidly being achieved inside the Community, and the external tariff a Community matter, it is becoming impossible to leave other forms of protection in national hands: quotas and all other protective measures need to be given a Community character.

Social policy

The social provisions of the Treaty (Articles 117–28) transfer few national powers to the Community, and the powers of the Council of Ministers (under Article 121) to assign specific tasks to the Commission to implement common measures of social policy have hardly been used. The Commission's role is mainly to encourage collaboration between member states. Apart from the important provisions on free movement of labour and social security for migrant workers (Articles 48–51), the Treaty does however allot two positive tasks to the Community institutions: the operation of a Social Fund to improve employment opportunities, and the implementation of a common policy for occupational training.

Social provisions

Member states agree in the Treaty on the need to promote improvement of the living and working conditions of labour. They consider that this will result not only from the operation of the Common Market, but also from the reduction of the gaps between legislative and administrative provisions (Article 117). The Commission has the task of promoting close cooperation between member states in the social field, especially on employment, labour legislation and working conditions, occupational training, social security, industrial health and safety, trade-union legislation and collective bargaining. It must act in close contact with member states, through studies, opinions and consultations (Article 118).

The Treaty bound the member states to ensure application of the principle of equal pay for men and women by the end of 1961 (Article 119). This date was subsequently postponed for three years, but despite substantial progress the principle had still not been fully applied in all the member countries by the end of 1966. Member states also undertake to endeavour to maintain the existing equivalence of paid holiday systems (Article 120).

The Social Fund

The Treaty sets up a Social Fund with the task of promoting employment opportunities and the mobility of labour (Article 123). It is administered by the Commission with the aid of a committee on which governments, trade unions and employers' organisations are represented (Article 124). At the request of a member state, the Fund can refund 50 per cent of expenditure incurred in reemploying workers by means of retraining and resettlement allowances, and in granting aids to make up the wages of workers temporarily laid off or put on short time when their factory is being converted to other production (Article 125).

A unanimous decision by the Council of Ministers is needed to continue these or any other operations by the Social Fund after the end of the transition period; the Council can however decide by qualified majority to end all or part of them (Article 126).

General principles for the implementation of a common occupational training policy were adopted in April 1963 in accordance with Article 128, but the Council has so far shown no signs of allowing the Commission to put them into practice. The Commission has also had no success in getting the Council to accept its proposals for extending the effectiveness of the Social Fund by allowing it to retrain workers before they become unemployed. Nor has the Council proved any more cooperative towards efforts to make practical moves towards harmonising the social policies of the Six.

The European Investment Bank

The Treaty establishes a European Investment Bank (Article 129), whose task is to contribute to balanced, steady development of the Common Market. By resorting to the capital market and to its own resources, and by granting loans and guarantees, it aids investments in the Community's less developed regions, the modernisation or conversion of firms, the establishment of new industry, and projects concerning several member states (Article 130). The Bank has a capital of $1,000 million, of which $250 million are paid up (Protocol on the Bank).

Under association agreements with Greece and Turkey and with eighteen African states (see below) the Bank can now grant loans within certain limits for projects in these countries, as well as in the six member states. By the end of 1966 the Bank's loans totalled $708·5 million, of which $357·2 million had been for projects in Southern Italy.

ASSOCIATION OF THE OVERSEAS COUNTRIES AND TERRITORIES

Under the Rome Treaty the Six agreed to associate with the Community the non-European countries and territories which had special relations with Belgium, France, Italy and the Netherlands, in order to aid their economic and social development and establish close relations between them and the Community as a whole (Article 131).

The objects to be pursued are: each member state should grant the associated countries and territories the same trade concessions which it grants to the other member states; the Six should contribute to the associated countries' and territories' investments and open tenders for Community-financed investments to firms in any member state or associated country or territory; subject to future agreement, the Treaty rules on right of establishment should apply in relations between the Six and the associated countries and territories (Article 132).

Duties on imports from the associated countries and territories into the Community are being reduced at the same rate as those on imports from other member states and will be completely eliminated by 1 July 1968. In principle the associated countries and territories should also abolish their customs duties on imports from the Six, but they may continue to impose duties needed for their development and industrialisation or for revenue purposes; there must however be no discrimination between member states in the level of such duties (Article 133).

The first five years of the association of the overseas countries were governed by an implementing Convention annexed to the Rome Treaty. This Convention set up the first European Development Fund, with resources of $581·25 million which were largely allotted over the five years 1958–62 as outright grants to aid social and economic development—mainly hospitals, schools, roads, harbours and water supply.

By the time the implementing Convention expired, all the associated African countries had achieved independence. All but Guinea freely chose to remain associated, however, and an entirely new and much more flexible five-year Convention, based on complete equality between the Six and their 18 partners, was signed in Yaoundé, capital of Cameroun, in July 1963. Under its terms the Six increased Community aid for social and economic development to the 18 to $730 million, of which $620 million were in the form of outright grants and $110 million in the form of loans; an additional $70 million were granted to associated countries still dependent. A feature of the Yaoundé Convention was that, of the total of $730 million granted for development, $230 million were to be for diversifying the associated countries' agricultural output, improving marketing and raising efficiency in farm production. The Yaoundé Convention also set up a Council of Association, with a permanent Association Committee, and a Parliamentary Conference; it provides for an Arbitration Tribunal in case of dispute.

A separate association agreement with Nigeria, signed in July 1966, follows similar lines to the Yaoundé Convention but in accordance with Nigeria's wishes does not provide for economic aid.

THE COMMUNITY INSTITUTIONS[1]

Institutional provisions

The institutions

The European Parliament. The Assembly, which adopted the title of European Parliament, has powers of discussion and control (Article 137). It is composed of 142 delegates chosen by and from the national parliaments: 36 each from France, Italy and Germany, 14 each from Belgium and the Netherlands, and 6 from Luxembourg (Article 138). The Treaty requires it (Article 138) to draw up projects for its election by direct universal suffrage by uniform procedure in all the member states; it submitted its projects to the Council of Ministers in 1960, but the Council, which can only decide unanimously in this field, had taken no action on them by the end of 1966, French opposition having proved unyielding.

The Parliament must hold an annual session on the third Tuesday of October and can hold other sessions at the request of a majority of its members, of the Council or of the Commission (Article 139). Members of the Commission can attend its sessions and address it, and the Commission must reply orally or in writing to questions from members; members of the Council also address the Parliament (Article 140) and hold an annual discussion with it. The Parliament normally acts by absolute majority of the votes cast (Article 141). It discusses in public session the annual report of the Commission and can force the Commission to resign collectively on a vote of censure passed by a two-thirds majority of the votes cast and an absolute majority of the Parliament's members (Articles 143 and 144).

The Council of Ministers. In the EEC the Council of Ministers takes all major policy decisions. To achieve the objectives of the Treaty it coordinates the general economic policies of the member states (Article 145). It is composed of representatives of the member states—one from each government—and the chairmanship is held for six months at a time by each member of the Council in rotation (Article 146). Except where the Treaty provides otherwise (see below, page 28), the Council takes its decisions by majority vote; for decisions requiring a qualified majority (i.e. almost all decisions) the votes of the member states are weighted as follows: France, Germany and Italy four each, Belgium and the Netherlands two each and Luxembourg one. Any twelve votes are sufficient to provide a qualified majority on a proposal of the Commission; for a decision not requiring a Commission proposal, (see below under *The Commission*), twelve votes are still necessary, but in this case they must represent at least four member states. Abstentions do not prevent the adoption of decisions requiring unanimity (Article 148).

For decisions on a Commission proposal the Council can amend the proposal by unanimous vote only; as long as the Council has not taken its decision, the Commission can modify its initial proposal (Article 149). It is this constant dialogue between Council and Commission on the proposals of the latter which forms the core of the Community's policy-making process.

Article 151 allows the Council to set up a body of permanent representatives. The Committee of Permanent Representatives set up in 1958 has assumed an important role as a continuing body preparing the Council's work and in fact taking many of the detailed decisions before formal approval by the Council.

The Council can ask the Commission to make any studies it requires, and to submit any suitable proposals (Article 152).

[1] See also 'The Structure of the European Community'.

The Commission. The Commission's task is to ensure the operation and development of the Common Market by seeing that the provisions of the Rome Treaty and all subsequent provisions based on it are carried out. It plays a major role in decision-making by formulating proposals on all policy matters and discussing them with the Council of Ministers, which takes the final decision. It can draw up recommendations or opinions on all matters covered by the Treaty, whether the Treaty expressly provides for them or not. It has powers of decision and takes part in the preparation of the acts of the Council and the Parliament (Article 155).

The Commission has nine members (Article 157) who reach their conclusions by simple majority vote (Article 163). They must all be nationals of member states, and there cannot be more than two nationals of any one member state. The members of the Commission must carry out their task in full independence in the general interest of the Community, and can neither request nor accept instructions from a government or other body. The member states for their part undertake not to seek to influence the Commission members in the execution of their task (Article 157).

The Commission members are appointed by agreement among the six governments for a four-year mandate, which can be renewed (Article 158). Normally, they remain in office until a successor has been appointed (Article 159). (Throughout 1966 the Commission remained in office under this provision, while the six governments failed to agree on the composition of a single Executive body for the three Communities.)

The president and two vice-presidents of the Commission are appointed, also by agreement among the governments, from among the Commission's nine members for a two-year renewable mandate (Article 161).

The Council and the Commission must consult each other, and organise by mutual agreement the methods of their collaboration (Article 162).

The European Court of Justice. The European Court of Justice, which ensures the respect of law in the interpretation and application of the Treaty (Article 164), is composed of seven judges, now organised in two chambers each of which deals with certain cases; it must however sit in plenary session for cases brought by a member state or a Community institution and for preliminary rulings under Article 177 (Article 165). The judges are assisted by two advocates-general who present in public their reasoned opinion—not committing the judges—on cases submitted to the Court (Article 166). The judges and advocates-general are appointed for six years by agreement among the governments and are eligible for reappointment; three and four judges alternately, and one advocate-general, are subject to renewal every three years; the judges appoint their president from among their number for a three-year renewable mandate (Article 167).

Appeals to the Court can be made by the Commission (Article 169) or, after they have called on the Commission to intervene, by the member states (Article 170), if they consider that a member state has not met one of its obligations under the Treaty. If the Court decides against a member state, the latter must take the steps necessary to implement the Court's judgment (Article 171). The Court can be—and normally is—given jurisdiction regarding penalties provided for in Community regulations (Article 172).

The Court is also the judge of the acts of the Council and the Commission, other than recommendations or opinions, and is competent to give judgment on appeals by a member state, the Council or the Commission on grounds of lack of authority, errors of substantial form, infringement of the Treaty or its implementing provisions, or abuse of power; any natural or legal person can also appeal, normally only within two months, against a decision addressed to him or directly concerning him (Article 173). The Court can declare the act null and void, or, in the case of regulations, indicate which parts of an annulled regulation should remain in force (Article 174). The member states and the other Community institutions, and legal and natural persons in the conditions set out above, can also bring cases against the Council or Commission for infringement of the Treaty through failure to act (Article 175). The institution whose act is rendered null and void or whose failure to act has been declared must take the necessary steps to carry out the Court's judgment (Article 176).

By way of preliminary rulings, the Court has power to decide on the interpretation of the Treaty, and the validity and interpretation of the acts of the Community institutions. National courts can—and, if they are courts from which there is no appeal, must—ask the Court of Justice for a ruling when these matters are in question (Article 177).

The Court is also competent in matters concerning damages caused by its institutions or officials (Article 178), disputes between the institutions and their staff (Article 179), matters concerning the European Investment Bank (Article 180), and contracts concluded by or for the Community (Article 181). Member states can ask it to arbitrate on differences between them (Article 182).

Appeals to the Court do not entail a stay of execution unless specifically granted by the Court (Article 185).

Provisions covering several institutions

To carry out their task the Council and the Commission issue regulations and directives, take decisions and draw up recommendations and opinions. Regulations are general in scope, binding in all respects and directly applicable in all the member states. Directives are binding as to the result to be achieved, but leave it to the member state to which they are addressed to decide on the form and means. Decisions are binding in all respects on those to whom they are addressed. Recommendations and opinions are not binding (Article 189).

Regulations, directives and decisions must be motivated (Article 190). Regulations must be published in the Communities' *Journal Officiel* and directives and decisions must be notified to those to whom they apply (Article 191). Decisions involving a pecuniary obligation on persons other than states are enforceable through the national authorities of the country concerned (Article 192).

The Economic and Social Committee

The Treaty sets up a consultative body called the Economic and Social Committee, consisting of 101 representatives of producers, farmers, workers, craftsmen, commerce, transport, the liberal professions and the general interest (Article 193). France, Germany and Italy have 24 members each, Belgium and the Netherlands 12 each and Luxembourg five; they are appointed in their personal capacity, for a four-year renewable mandate, by unanimous vote of the Council (Articles 194 and 195). The Committee must be consulted by the Council or by the Commission in certain matters specified in the Treaty, and whenever these institutions think fit (Article 198).

FINANCING THE COMMUNITY

The Community's receipts and expenditure must be presented as estimates for each financial year and previously authorised in an annual budget (Article 199). Provisionally, its resources are furnished directly by the member states in the following proportions (per cent):

| | General Budget[1] | Social Fund[1] | European Agricultural Fund[2] | | |
			1965/6	1966/7	1 July 1967 onwards[3]
Belgium	7·9	8·8	7·95	7·95	8·1
France	28	32	32·58	29·26	32
Germany	28	32	31·67	30·83	31·2
Italy	28	20	18	22	20·3
Luxembourg	0·2	0·2	0·22	0·22	0·2
Netherlands	7·9	7	9.58	9.74	8·2

[1] EEC Treaty, Article 200.
[2] Decision of Council of Ministers, 11 May 1966.
[3] From 1 July 1967 until December 1969 these contributions will cover the cost of only about 55 per cent of the Agricultural Fund's expenditure, the remainder being covered by the levies on imports of farm produce, 90 per cent of which sums will be handed over to the Fund.

The Commission is, however, bound under the Treaty to present proposals to the Council for replacement of the member states' contributions by direct Community revenues, notably the receipts from the common external tariff (Article 201). It presented proposals to this end in April 1965; they had not been fully discussed, however, before the French government began its seven-month boycott of the Community institutions in July of that year, and have since been in abeyance. Nevertheless, 90 per cent of the levies on imports of agricultural products will be paid direct to the Agricultural Guidance and Guarantee Fund (usually known as FEOGA, its initials in French) from 1 July 1967 onwards and the full yield from 1 January 1970 onwards (Regulation No. 25 of April 1962 and Council decisions of 11 May 1966).

This is bound to raise again before 1970 the questions of allocating to the Community as direct revenue the import duties on industrial goods also, and of democratic control over the large sums which will be under Community administration (between $1,400 and $1,500 million annually for agriculture alone, and about $300 million for other purposes).

Budget credits are inscribed for a single year but can be carried over to the next year (Article 202); the budgetary year is from 1 January to 31 December (Article 203). The Commission's draft budget must be forwarded to the Council by 30 September of the preceding year, and the Council must submit it, with any amendments, to the European Parliament by 31 October. The Council adopts the budget by qualified majority (Article 203). The budget accounts are audited by a Control Commission of qualified, independent auditors (Article 206) and drawn up in units of account at present equivalent to a US dollar (Article 207).

GENERAL AND FINAL PROVISIONS

The Community has legal personality (Article 210), and its legal capacity in member states is the most extensive accorded to legal persons by their national legislation (Article 211). To carry out the tasks given it by the

Treaty, the Commission can gather any information and carry out any checks, within limits set by the Council in accordance with the Rome Treaty provisions (Article 213).

The Six undertook by the Treaty to engage in negotiations to ensure for their nationals: the protection of persons, and the enjoyment and protection of their rights throughout the Community in the same conditions that each state grants to its own nationals; the elimination of double taxation within the Community; mutual recognition of companies so as to allow them to keep their legal personality if they move their place of registration from one Community country to another, and to merge with companies in other Community countries; simplification of formalities for reciprocal recognition and execution of judicial decisions and arbitration awards (Article 220). Much has been achieved in these fields, but no decision had been reached by the end of 1966 on the establishment of a legal framework for 'European companies' and the coordination of company law in the member countries, or on a draft European patent convention.

National security: emergencies. The Treaty provisions cannot force a member state to supply information which it considers against its vital interests to divulge, or prevent a member state from taking steps it considers vital to its security (Article 223). Should a member state be called on to take action in case of serious internal disturbances, war or the threat of war, or in order to uphold peace or international security, the member states consult on ways of avoiding adverse effects on the operation of the Common Market (Article 224). Should a member state experience serious difficulties in an industry or region, it can ask the Commission to authorise safeguard measures to restore the situation and adapt the sector concerned to the Common Market economy. Such measures may include derogation from Treaty rules for a strictly limited period (Article 226). The Treaty provisions apply to European territories whose foreign affairs are in the charge of a member state (Article 227).

Relations between the EEC and other countries. Any agreements envisaged under the Treaty between the Community and other states or international organisations are negotiated by the Commission and concluded by the Council; they are binding on member states (Article 228). The Commission is responsible for maintaining all necessary contacts with the United Nations and its specialised agencies and with GATT (Article 229); the Community also cooperates with the Council of Europe and the OECD (Articles 230, 231).

Treaty amendment. The Council can authorise by unanimous vote provisions for action needed to achieve one of the Community's objectives but not provided for in the Treaty (Article 235). Treaty amendments can be proposed by a member state or the Commission; if the proposal is approved by the Council after consulting the European Parliament, a conference of the member governments meets with a view to working out the necessary modifications by mutual agreement. Any modifications agreed then require ratification by the member governments before being adopted (Article 236).

New members: association. Any European state can apply to become a member of the Community. If the Council, having consulted the Commission, is unanimously in agreement, the conditions of admission and adaptations of the Treaty are the object of an agreement between the member states and the state applying; this agreement requires ratification by all member states (Article 237). The Community can also conclude with other countries or groups of countries association agreements involving reciprocal rights and obligations and joint actions; such agreements are concluded by the Council acting unanimously (Article 238).

Duration. The Treaty is concluded for an unlimited period (Article 240).

PROCEDURE: MAJORITY VOTING AND UNANIMITY

The procedures laid down by the Rome Treaty are described in detail later in this book ('The Structure of the European Community'). All the sections of the Treaty in fact give detailed indications of the procedure to be applied: whether regulations, directives, decisions, recommendations or opinions are to be issued, whether the European Parliament and the Economic and Social Committee are to be consulted, and whether the Council of Ministers is to take its decisions by qualified majority or unanimous vote.

For policy decisions the procedure is, in broad outline, as follows. The Commission makes proposals and, usually after consulting the European Parliament and the Economic and Social Committee, and after exhaustive discussion in the Council between the member states and with the Commission, the Council of Ministers takes its decision. Since the beginning of 1966, the Council has been able to take its decisions on most matters by qualified majority vote. From the end of the transition period onwards, the number of subjects for which unanimity is required is reduced still further. Even on such important matters as external trade, a decision will be possible, under the Rome Treaty, by qualified majority vote; the French government, however, made it clear in Luxembourg in January 1966 that it does not agree with its Treaty obligations on majority voting and that, in its view, discussion on very important issues must go on until unanimous agreement is reached.

On a number of vital questions, however, unanimity is still required under the Treaty after the end of the transition period. These matters are listed below:

—Modifications or extensions of the common external tariff, except for temporary suspensions or reductions not exceeding 20 per cent of the duty rate (Article 28).

—Extension to nationals of a non-member state of the unrestricted right to supply services (Article 59).

—Coordination of exchange-rate policy concerned with capital movements (Article 70).

—Features of the common transport policy which might 'seriously affect living standards and employment in certain regions and also the utilisation of transport equipment' (Article 75).

—Whether, to what extent, and how Community measures should be taken for sea and air transport (Article 84).

—The authorisation of state aids banned under Article 92 (Article 93).

—Harmonisation of legislation on turnover tax, excise duties and other indirect taxes (Article 99).

—The alignment of member countries' existing legislation (Article 100).

—Measures of economic policy—but not the implementing directives for such measures (Article 103).

—The granting of tasks to the Commission in connection with the implementation of joint measures in the social policy field (Article 121).

—Continuation of the operation of the Social Fund after the end of the transition period (Article 126).

—Conventions on free movement for workers of the associated overseas countries and territories (Article 135). This requires the unanimous agreement of the member states themselves and not of the Council of Ministers.

—Adoption of arrangements for direct elections to the European Parliament (Article 138). Strictly speaking under the Treaty (Article 8) this should be done by the end of the transition period.

—Changes in the number of members of the Commission (Article 157), the number of judges (Article 165) or advocates-general (Article 166) at the Court, or in the agreed official and working languages (Article 217).

—Appointment of the members of the Commission (Article 158) and of the Court of Justice (Article 167). These appointments are made not by the Council but by the governments of the member states in mutual agreement.

—Nomination of the Economic and Social Committee (Article 193) and of the Audit Commission (Article 206).

—Provisions for the Community to have its own direct financial resources (Article 201). Under Article 8, this should be decided before the end of the transition period.

—Alterations in the list of products (arms, munitions, war materials) excluded from the Treaty provisions for reasons of national military security (Article 223).

—Provisions for action needed to achieve one of the Community's objectives but for which powers are not envisaged in the Treaty (Article 235).

—Admission of new members (Article 237). Subsequent conditions of admission and adaptations of the Treaty are to be objects of agreement between the member states and the applying state, and they require ratification by all the contracting states.

—Conclusion of association agreements (Article 238).

THE STRUCTURE OF THE EUROPEAN COMMUNITY

TONY BURGESS

THE BEGINNINGS

THE European Community may be defined as an organisation set up by a group of Western European countries with the aim of achieving eventual political union through a gradual process of practical economic integration. Although the potential of the Community may have been accepted at the best only tacitly, and as a very long-term objective, by some of the signatories of the founding Treaties, the undoubted intention of the men who drafted these documents was to establish an institutional framework which could develop, by a process of evolution, into a viable system of government for a European federation, possibly a United States of Europe.

The Treaties themselves, however, were never intended to be much more than formal statements of mutually accepted principles—skeletons needing the flesh and sinew of detailed legislation to give them life. In the sense therefore that the emerging shape of the European Community has depended, and will continue to depend, on the manner in which its member countries choose to interpret the broadly defined aims of its founders—the manner in which they choose to pad out the skeleton—it is an evolutionary growth. Even the Community's institutions themselves have to a certain extent developed empirically, and in several instances they have been able to reinterpret their terms of reference to meet new or changing situations.

Membership of the European Community is at present confined to the six original signatory states of the founding Treaties—Belgium, France, the Federal Republic of Germany, Italy, Luxembourg and the Netherlands—although its architects' intentions were that membership should be open to any European state willing to accept the obligations of the Treaties. In the event, however, the British application for entry failed when in January 1963 France exercised the veto which all existing members possess over the admission of new members, ostensibly because President de Gaulle was not satisfied that the United Kingdom was prepared to accept the spirit of the Treaties (see the chapter entitled 'Britain and the European Community'). Following the failure of the British negotiations, the applications for membership which had been lodged by Ireland, Denmark and Norway were not pursued by these countries.

So far, for simplicity, we have referred to 'the European Community', but the use of the singular is strictly inaccurate since there are in fact three separate European Communities: the European Coal and Steel Community (ECSC), the European Economic Community (EEC, more frequently known as the Common Market), and the European Atomic Energy Community (Euratom). Membership of the three Communities is identical, consisting of the six countries listed above, and although there are certain constitutional differences between the three organisations, particularly between ECSC on the one hand and EEC and Euratom on the other, similar basic principles are embodied in all three founding Treaties, and each Community has a similar institutional structure. The plans, already far advanced, for merging these three Communities into a single constitutional entity are described at the end of this chapter.

The establishment of the first of the three Communities, the European Coal and Steel Community, resulted from the Schuman Declaration of 9 May 1950. In this declaration Robert Schuman, then French foreign minister, proposed that the coal and steel resources of France and Germany should be pooled in an organisation open to all European countries. The invitation was accepted by the governments of Germany, Italy, Belgium, Luxembourg and the Netherlands, but the British government replied that it would 'reluctantly be unable to accept . . . a commitment to pool resources and set up an authority with certain sovereign powers as a prior condition to joining talks. . . .'

The aims of ECSC, which began to operate in 1953 under the terms of the Paris Treaty, were twofold. In the first place it was intended that the pooling of French and German basic production would achieve the final reconciliation of these two traditional enemies by making further conflict between them impossible on practical grounds. Secondly, ECSC was conceived as the first step towards a new political order in Europe. Out of limited economic integration its founders hoped that political unity would grow. Their choice of a gradualist approach—an attempt to create practical solidarity between European countries through concrete achievements in closely defined fields—was conditioned by disillusionment over previous attempts to unite Europe in one move under more grandiose but basically impractical designs.

The initial success of ECSC, under the leadership of Jean Monnet, who had played a major part in drafting the Schuman Declaration, led very quickly to the first attempt at political union in Europe. Shortly after the signature of the ECSC Treaty, the Community governments signed the European Defence Community (EDC) Treaty, which, by placing the six countries' military resources under joint control, would have solved the problem of German rearmament. At the same time a plan for a European Political Community was drawn up. These plans came to nothing, however, when the EDC Treaty, ratified by the other five parliaments, was rejected by the French National Assembly.

This failure notwithstanding, the logic of European economic integration, rapidly demonstrated by ECSC, was not to be denied, and the six governments, by their decision to extend the process to the whole field covered by their separate national economies, showed that they had drawn the obvious conclusion. As a result, they concluded two further treaties, the Rome Treaties, setting up the European Economic Community (which rapidly took to itself the title of the Common Market, although the earlier Paris Treaty already referred to 'the common market for coal and steel') and the European Atomic Energy Community. The aim of EEC, which with Euratom came into being on 1 January 1958, was to ensure the continued economic expansion of the member countries, and thereby the steady social progress of their peoples, by the creation of a single market for all goods and factors of production in place of the six separate national markets. The

Community governments also recognised that the establishment of the thoroughgoing customs union which they envisaged would entail the complete integration of their national economic policies over a very wide front.

Euratom's main aim, given the enormous cost of nuclear research which often places a severe strain on the resources of even major countries acting alone, was to ensure the efficient development of a nuclear industry on a Community-wide basis, to the point where it would be capable of making a major competitive contribution to Europe's rapidly expanding power needs. Euratom also concerns itself with medical and biological research in the nuclear field and the industrial uses of atomic energy, but under the terms of the Treaty its functions are strictly limited to the peaceful uses of the atom.

THE MAIN INSTITUTIONAL FRAMEWORK

The institutions of the European Community (the reversion to the singular is here deliberate in view of the functional interdependence of the three legally distinct Communities) were constituted by the founding Treaties in such a way as to form the basis of a system of government for a Europe ultimately politically united along federal lines. The system already contains an embryonic legislature (the three Councils of Ministers, the Executives in their policy-making rôle and the European Parliament), a civil service (the Executives in their administrative rôle and their ancillary bodies), and a judiciary (the European Court of Justice). Although considerable development of these bodies' powers, and clearer definition of their functions in relation to each other and to the member governments, will be required before they can fairly be described as a viable system of federal government, the potential exists in the Treaties, as the men who drafted them intended that it should. This potential has been clearly recognised and endorsed by most of the statesmen and administrators who have been responsible for implementing the Treaties.

The Councils of Ministers

Until such time as the merger of the three Communities, or at least of their institutions, is achieved, there are legally three separate Councils of Ministers, one for each of the existing Communities. The Councils are made up of ministerial representatives from each member country. In theory the actual ministers taking part in any particular meeting of the Council vary with the subjects under discussion—ministers of transport when transport policy is on the agenda, ministers of agriculture to discuss farm problems, and so on—but in practice all major Community decisions are taken by a Council consisting of the six countries' foreign ministers. Since the same persons often take part in meetings of the three different Councils of Ministers, the distinction between these legally separate bodies has tended to become blurred in the minds of observers not intimately connected with Community affairs. Nevertheless, considerable differences exist between the competence of the ECSC Council on the one hand, and the EEC and Euratom Councils on the other.

Ministers taking part in meetings of the Councils do so as the official representatives of their countries, and a major function of the Councils is to ensure that the varying national interests of the member countries are fully taken into account in the shaping of Community policy.

The decision-taking machinery set up by the Treaties founding the three Communities is based on the acceptance of weighted majority voting in the

Councils of Ministers as the norm of Community practice. A unanimous vote is required only where a specific exception to this principle is made in the Treaty concerned. In practice, these exceptions may be divided into two groups. There are a few permanent exceptions, of which decisions on the admission of new members and on amendments to the Treaties themselves are the most important, and, in the case of the EEC and Euratom, a much larger group of temporary exceptions, applicable during the initial stages of these two Communities.

The temporary exemptions from the principle of majority voting under the two Rome Treaties are all meant to terminate at or before the end of the EEC's transition period, i.e. by 1970 at the latest. Some EEC decisions initially requiring a unanimous vote were transferred to the realm of majority voting when the Common Market moved into the second stage of its transition period in January 1962, and most of the remaining temporary exceptions were removed when the Community moved into the third stage of its transition period at the beginning of 1966. The so-called 'gentlemen's agreement' on majority voting—that a majority vote would not be used in practice to override the vital national interests of any member country—which ended the Community crisis of the second half of 1965 and early 1966 does not affect the basic Treaty position on this issue.

The Rome Treaties lay down that where decisions of the EEC or Euratom Councils of Ministers require only a majority vote, the votes of the member countries shall have the following weights: France, Germany and Italy, four votes each; Belgium and the Netherlands, two votes each; Luxembourg, one vote. Of this total of seventeen votes, any twelve votes are sufficient to carry a decision based on a proposal put forward by an Executive (see below). Where a decision is being taken on a matter that does not require a prior proposal from the relevant Executive, these twelve favourable votes must be spread among at least four member states. The latter provision ensures that when the Council is not acting on a proposal of the Executive, the three smaller Community countries cannot be outvoted as a group by the three larger countries. In these circumstances the minimum consensus required would be two of the larger countries plus Belgium and the Netherlands.

In the Paris Treaty, which gave the ECSC Council of Ministers more limited powers than those later bestowed on the ministerial bodies of the EEC and Euratom (see below under *The Formulation of Community Policy*), there are no temporary exceptions to the general principle of qualified majority voting. There are, however, a number of permanent exceptions concerned with matters outside the strict coal and steel sectors. Also the system of weighting votes is rather different, being conditional on the relative importance of the member countries as coal and steel producers.

The chairmanships of the Councils of Ministers are exercised in rotation by the ministerial representatives of each member country, for periods of three months in the case of ECSC and of six months in the case of EEC and Euratom.

Although the Councils of Ministers themselves are non-continuous bodies, meeting at intervals, their sessions are prepared, in the case of the EEC and Euratom, by a Committee of Permanent Representatives of the member countries, and, in the case of ECSC, by a Coordinating Committee. Both the Permanent Representatives Committee and the Coordinating Committee are made up of the member governments' ambassadors to the Communities, and operate on a continuing basis. Each Council is also serviced by a full-time secretariat.

The Community Executives

The executive bodies of the three Communities—called the Commission in EEC and Euratom, and the High Authority in ECSC—have become, partly as a result of the responsibilities given them under the Treaties and partly as a result of their own initiatives, the mainsprings of all action at the Community level. The histories of the three Communities since their inception have been largely the history of these three bodies' attempts to translate the ideal of European unity into practice.

The individual characteristics of the three separate Executives are described below, but they each have the same overriding responsibility— to act as the guardians of the principles contained in the founding Treaties and to represent and safeguard the interests of their respective Communities as entities. In this latter task the responsibilities of the Executives are in clear distinction from those of the Councils of Ministers, where the interests of each member country are represented. To ensure that the Executives act only in the interests of the Community as a whole, their members undertake not to be swayed by the national interests of their own countries, and pledge themselves to independence of their governments, from whom they may not receive instructions. The deliberations of each Executive are secret, and decisions are taken on a straight majority vote. The Executives operate on the collegiate principle, and a decision once reached binds the Executive concerned as a body.

Each Executive has its own staff, forming the nucleus of a fully comprehensive international civil service, members of which are responsible only to their respective Executive, not to the national administrations of their own countries. The Executives are continuous bodies, the duties of whose members and staff occupy them on a full-time basis.

The High Authority of ECSC is composed of nine members, with its headquarters in Luxembourg and a total staff of about 1,000. Decisions of the High Authority are directly binding on the coal, steel, iron-ore and ferrous scrap industries of the Six, without the need for these decisions to be embodied in national legislation. The initial task of the High Authority, when ECSC was first set up, was to establish a common market for these products throughout the geographical area of the Six. This it did by abolishing all trade barriers for these products between the member countries, and by removing trade distortions such as discriminatory pricing of coal or steel based on the nationality of the buyer, unjustified government subsidies to national industries, and other impediments to rational patterns of trade.

Once a single Community-wide market for ECSC products had been established, the main emphasis of the High Authority's work changed from that of innovation to the administration of the system which it had created. It is now principally concerned with supervising the efficient operation of the common market for coal and steel products, ensuring that the Paris Treaty rules on fair competition between firms are observed, enforcing Community anti-trust legislation to prevent any firm or group of firms from attaining or abusing a dominant market position, encouraging investment and research in the Community coal and steel industries, and offsetting the social effects of the changing patterns of employment in the European coal and steel industries. The latter task has become more urgent in recent years as a result of the diminishing importance of the European coal industry, and High Authority action in this field has taken two main forms: material assistance to new industries who show interest in setting up in declining coal-mining areas, and retraining schemes and financial assistance for former workers in

ECSC industries who may be obliged to seek jobs in new industries or new areas.

Eight members of the High Authority are appointed, on the basis of unanimous agreement, by the member governments. The ninth member, who has come traditionally to be regarded as the representative of trade union interests in the High Authority, is coopted by the other eight. Each member holds office for six years, and is eligible for reappointment. One-third of the membership of the High Authority is renewed or reappointed every two years, and for this regular renewal half the members are named by cooption. Not more than two members of the body may be of the same nationality. The president and vice-president of the High Authority are appointed by the governments, on a unanimous vote, from among the members. They hold office for two years, but may be reappointed.

The Common Market Commission is also composed of nine members, with its headquarters in Brussels and a total staff of about three thousand. The main task of the Commission is to ensure the implementation of the Rome Treaty and to supervise the gradual integration of the entire economies of the six member countries, a process which involves the removal of unjustified restrictions on the free movement of goods, capital, services and labour, and the working out of common policies in sectors such as agriculture, transport and external trade. In carrying out this task, the Commission has two distinct roles—as an initiator responsible for putting forward proposals for new Community action, and as an administrative body responsible for putting into effect policy decisions already adopted by the Council of Ministers. The first of these two roles is examined more closely below under the heading *The Formulation of Community Policy*.

All nine members of the EEC Commission are appointed unanimously by the national governments. Members hold office for four years, and are eligible for reappointment; their terms of office are concurrent. Not more than two members of the Commission may be of the same nationality. The president and two vice-presidents of the Commission are appointed from among the members by the six governments acting unanimously. Their terms of office are for two years, but they may be reappointed. In the event of the six governments failing to agree on the replacement or reappointment of a member or officer of the Commission when the individual's term has expired, the person concerned remains in office until such agreement is reached. (This condition applies also to members of the other two Community Executives.)

The Euratom Commission comprises five members. Its headquarters are in Brussels, and it has a staff of about two-and-a-half thousand research workers and seven hundred administrative officials. Its task is to ensure the establishment within the Community of a viable and efficient industry for the peaceful exploitation of nuclear resources, to encourage nuclear research and the training of atomic scientists, to administer the Supply Agency through which all nuclear fuel used in the Community's civilian atomic industry is channelled, to supervise the common market for all nuclear materials and equipment which has been set up among the Six, and to lay down safety standards for the Community's nuclear industry as a whole.

In certain cases the Euratom Commission can issue regulations which are directly binding on Community firms operating in the nuclear field, and it has wide powers of inspection and control over the use of nuclear materials which pass through the Supply Agency's hands, to make sure that they are being used only for specified and peaceful purposes.

All five members of the Euratom Commission are appointed unanimously by the six governments, hold office for four years, and are eligible for re-appointment. Their terms of office are concurrent; no two members of the Commission may be of the same nationality. The president and vice-president are appointed under the same conditions as the officers of the EEC Commission.

The European Parliament

The Paris Treaty, which established the European Coal and Steel Community, made provision for a Parliamentary Assembly 'consisting of representatives of the peoples of the member states of the Community', which would exercise democratic supervision over the actions of the High Authority. When the Common Market and Euratom were set up, this Assembly, which became known as the European Parliament, was given the responsibility of democratic supervision over all three Communities. At the present time it has no real legislative power, but it has made full and vigorous use of the rights of consultation covering a wide range of Community activity granted to it under the Treaties.

The Parliament consists of 142 members, delegated by the national legislatures of the six Community countries. France, Germany and Italy send thirty-six members each; Belgium and the Netherlands fourteen members each; and Luxembourg six members. The composition of the groups of delegates from the various countries reflects the broad balance of the parties in the national parliaments concerned, although Communists and members of extreme right-wing parties are not admitted to the European Parliament. Eventual election of the European Parliament by direct, Community-wide suffrage is envisaged in the Treaties, but this provision has not yet been implemented.

Perhaps the most significant aspect of the way in which the Parliament operates is the fact that its members have decided, of their own accord, to sit as political groups, not as national delegations. The three main political divisions which have emerged in the Parliament are Christian Democrat, Socialist and Liberal. There are also now a small number of French Gaullist members.

The Parliament meets in Strasbourg, and holds about ten full sessions a year, of a week each. Its specialised Standing Committees, each of which closely follows a specific aspect of the activities of the Community Executives, meet more frequently.

The Community Executives are obliged to submit annual reports to the Parliament, which can force the resignation of any of the Executives as a body on a two-thirds vote of censure. The Parliament has the right to be consulted before certain types of decisions are taken by EEC and Euratom. It also has the right to scrutinise the three Communities' budgets, and its members may put written questions to the three Executives. Representatives of the Executives and of the Councils of Ministers are entitled to address the Parliament under certain conditions at their own request.

The Parliament elects its president and officers from among its members. Except in special circumstances laid down in the Treaties, the Parliament acts by means of an absolute majority of the votes cast. The full sessions of the Parliament are held in public.

The European Court of Justice

The European Court of Justice is the final point of appeal on all matters concerning the interpretation or application of the Community Treaties.

It has the sole power to rule on the legality of acts committed by the Councils of Ministers and the Community Executives. It can decide on appeals for exemption from Community regulations, questions of Community procedure, disputes over interpretation of the Treaties or their implementing regulations, and cases where Community institutions are alleged to have exceeded their powers. It may also judge cases where one of the Executives or a member government is alleged to have failed to carry out its responsibilities under the Treaties.

Right of appeal to the Court is open to member governments and to Community institutions. Under the Common Market and Euratom Treaties, private individuals or legal persons may also appeal to the Court against Community rules which are directed at them, or which concern them directly or specifically. The ECSC Treaty allows firms or associations of firms subject to the Treaty's provisions to appeal against particular Community decisions which concern them, or against general decisions which they feel result in injustice when applied in their case.

The Court may also give judgment and award damages in cases where the plaintiff claims that he has suffered loss as a result of an act of a Community institution. Under certain circumstances the Court may also decide preliminary issues submitted by national courts in Community countries, where questions of the interpretation of the Treaties or the validity of Community decisions are raised in domestic litigation.

The judgments of the Court have direct force of law in all Community countries, without the prior need to be incorporated in the member countries' legislation. They are binding on all parties concerned, whether individuals, firms, national governments, or Community institutions. In the twelve years of the Court's history, there has been no occasion on which its decisions have been resisted by member governments, or on which a government has refused to carry out its rulings.

The Court, which meets in Luxembourg, consists of seven Judges, appointed unanimously by the member governments from among persons of high legal standing in their own countries. The Judges are assisted by two Advocates General, also appointed by the governments, and a Clerk appointed by the Court. The Judges serve for terms of six years, and may be reappointed. Partial renewal of the membership of the Court occurs every three years, affecting three and four Judges alternately. The Judges elect from among their number a President of the Court, who holds office for three years.

The Court is divided into two chambers of three Judges each. Decisions are reached through deliberations in either of the two chambers or in full court. A simple majority of the Judges is sufficient for the adoption of a ruling. No dissenting opinions are published.

The Formulation of Community Policy

The differences between the Paris Treaty founding ECSC and the later Rome Treaties founding EEC and Euratom are most clearly apparent in the provisions which each makes for the formulation of Community policy.

In ECSC the executive body, the High Authority, has considerably greater powers of direct action than were later given to the EEC and Euratom Commissions. The role of the ECSC Council of Ministers is confined over a large field of Community activity to putting forward the opinions of the governments before the High Authority takes decisions which will be binding on the coal and steel industries of the six countries. However, the Council's prior approval, based on either a simple or a qualified majority vote, depending on the issue, is required for most important decisions. With minor exceptions, unanimous approval by the Council is necessary only for matters outside the strict coal and steel sectors.

In the Common Market and Euratom, there is a far greater degree of interdependence between the Executives and the Councils of Ministers in the process of defining Community policy. In these two Communities the Councils of Ministers take the final policy decisions, although they can do so only on the basis of proposals put forward by the Commission of the Community concerned. The Councils can only modify such proposals by a unanimous vote, even in cases where a majority vote is sufficient to adopt the particular proposal as it stands. In EEC and Euratom, therefore, the Commissions have almost the sole right to propose Community policy, while the Councils of Ministers retain responsibility for the ultimate decisions on these proposals. Only in certain limited circumstances do the EEC and Euratom Commissions have the right to take independent action, usually in their administrative role in the implementation of policy already adopted in principle, or under a specific mandate from the Council.

In the process of making proposals for Community action, the EEC and Euratom Commissions possess one important faculty which has greatly facilitated agreement in the Council of Ministers in the past on a number of difficult issues. The Executive concerned has the right to modify its proposals at any time up to the moment when the Council actually reaches a decision. After observing the way in which the debate has gone in the Council on a contested issue, and taking account of the various national positions, the Executive may therefore produce a compromise solution at the psychological moment—a 'package deal' in Community jargon.

Under the Rome Treaties the Economic and Social Committee (see below under *Ancillary Community Bodies*) and the European Parliament have the right to be consulted before most Community decisions are adopted. The Consultative Committee of the ECSC (see below) has the same right in many circumstances in the formulation of ECSC policy.

Ancillary Community Bodies

The three Executives and the Councils of Ministers are advised before formulating or implementing Community policy by a number of specialised or general committees. Some of these committees were envisaged in the Treaties, others have been set up on an *ad hoc* basis as the need arose.

The Economic and Social Committee, consisting of 101 members representing employers' organisations, trade unions, consumers' associations and other social and economic groups, has the right to advise the Common Market and Euratom Commissions and Councils of Ministers on many aspects of Community policy.

The Consultative Committee, consisting of fifty-one members, performs a similar task for the ECSC High Authority.

The Scientific and Technical Committee, made up of twenty-one independent nuclear experts, advises the Euratom Commission on nuclear problems. This is a purely advisory body, and its members have no official status as representatives of their countries, but it does have the right to be consulted on certain issues.

The Transport Committee, consisting of independent experts appointed by the Council of Ministers, advises the Common Market Commission on transport problems.

In addition to the above bodies, five particularly important committees have been set up within the framework of EEC to facilitate coordination of the member countries' economic policies and to speed cooperation between them in the vital monetary and financial spheres. The first of these committees, the Monetary Committee, was specifically envisaged in the Rome Treaty. The rest were established as the increasing pace and scope of economic integration in the Community made them necessary.

The Monetary Committee, made up of the EEC Commission and national experts, advises the Commission and Council of Ministers on a wide range of monetary-policy questions, including the coordination of Community policy on world monetary problems. One of the Committee's main functions is to bring together the officials of the six countries responsible for drafting national monetary policy.

The Short-Term Economic Policy Committee was set up in 1960, and modelled directly on the Monetary Committee. As its name indicates, its purpose is to facilitate the coordination of the member countries' short-term economic policies, with particular reference to the avoidance of cyclical fluctuations.

The Budgetary Policy Committee, with the Medium-Term Economic Policy Committee and the Committee of Governors of Central Banks (see below), was set up under a series of decisions taken by the Common Market Council of Ministers in April 1964. The aim of these decisions was to extend the process of economic integration between the Six to coordination of their medium-term policies, and to strengthen their existing monetary and financial cooperation. The Budgetary Committee groups senior government officials, and has the task of coordinating the member countries' budgetary policies and of advising the Common Market Commission on all problems in this field.

The Medium-Term Economic Policy Committee, composed of senior officials of the six governments, advises the Common Market Commission and Council of Ministers on the coordination of the member countries' economic policies over periods of four to five years. This committee supplements the work of the Monetary and Short-Term Economic Policy Committees.

The Committee of Governors of the Central Banks was set up to harmonise the policies of the Community countries' central banks.

In addition to the committees listed above, whose principal role is to provide expert advice for the Community Executives, Councils of Ministers and member governments on a wide range of economic, social and technical problems, four funds have been set up to promote investment in the Community and its associated countries, and to offset where necessary the social cost of economic progress. The first three of these funds listed below are administered by the Common Market Commission; only the last, the European Investment Bank, has a separate legal existence.

The European Social Fund has the task of preventing or alleviating any social hardship which might result from structural changes in the Community economy brought about by closer economic integration. In particular, the Fund promotes employment opportunities, especially in areas where traditional industries are declining, and facilitates the mobility of workers within the Community. Like the readaptation aid provided by the ECSC High Authority, the Social Fund assists workers who have had to move or change their jobs by providing vocational retraining, and resettlement and other grants. Its method of operation is to refund fifty per cent of the expenditure undertaken by the member governments for these purposes.

The Agricultural Guidance and Guarantee Fund, set up under EEC's common agricultural policy, has three tasks: to help finance modernisation schemes and structural improvements in the Community's farm sector, to undertake support buying of agricultural produce on the Community market when prices fall below those guaranteed to farmers, and to provide rebates on Community exports of farm produce when world market prices are below the Community guaranteed minimum.

The European Development Fund administers the bulk of the development aid which the Community as an entity (as distinct from member countries individually) provides for eighteen associated African countries.

The European Investment Bank, with independent status as an international financial institution, encourages investment in the economically less developed areas of the Community and helps to finance modernisation schemes or new projects of general Community interest. The largest proportion of the Bank's loans to date have been made to promote the industrialisation of Southern Italy, the Community's economically most backward area. Recently the Bank has also begun to finance development projects in countries having association agreements with the Community.

The organs of association

In addition to the Association Convention between the EEC and eighteen independent African states,[1] the Common Market also has separate Association Agreements with Greece and Turkey. Each of these arrangements has its own institutional structure consisting of a Council of Association, a Parliamentary Conference, and a Judicial Tribunal.

The three Councils of Association comprise representatives of the Common Market Council of Ministers and the Commission on the one hand and representatives of the associated partner on the other (one representative from each of the eighteen countries in the case of the African Convention). Since the Association Councils are ministerial bodies meeting only periodically, detailed day-to-day administration of each agreement is delegated to Association Committees meeting at government-official level.

The Parliamentary Conferences, which usually meet once a year to consider their respective Association Councils' annual reports, group members of the European Parliament and parliamentarians from the associated countries. Judicial Tribunals have been set up under each agreement to settle legal disputes between the parties.

The UK–ECSC Association Agreement, signed in December 1954, set up a Council of Association comprising British and High Authority representatives, which meets regularly at ministerial and expert level. The aims of the Association are to lower trade barriers in coal and steel products between Britain and the ECSC, to promote the coordination of economic policies affecting these products, and to further cooperation in the fields of technology, science and industrial hygiene.

The common services of the Executives

Three specialised service departments have been set up jointly by the three Community Executives.

[1] Burundi, Cameroun, Central African Republic, Chad, Congo (Brazzaville), Congo (Democratic Republic), Dahomey, Gabon, Ivory Coast, Madagascar, Mali, Mauritania, Niger, Rwanda, Senegal, Somali Republic, Togo, Upper Volta. Nigeria signed a trade agreement with the EEC in 1966.

The Legal Service advises the Executives on all legal matters, from the drafting of Community legislation to issues raised before the Community Court of Justice.

The European Communities Statistical Office is responsible for the collection and compilation of comparable statistics for each of the Community countries, and for the production of statistics covering the Community as a whole. The Office publishes a wide range of monthly, quarterly and annual statistical summaries, and many special reports.

The European Communities Press and Information Service deals with all aspects of public information work and press liaison in the Community countries and abroad. London, Washington and New York are among the cities outside the Community in which the Service maintains information offices.

THE COMMUNITY BUDGETS

The European Coal and Steel Community is the only one of the three Communities which currently has an independent source of revenue. This derives from a levy which the High Authority is empowered, under the Paris Treaty, to impose on the annual turnover of all firms in the Community coal, steel and associated industries. At the present time this levy is fixed at 0.25 per cent of turnover.

Up to now the budgets of EEC and Euratom have been derived from direct contributions by the member governments, although it is envisaged that these two Communities will eventually acquire independent revenues based on the proceeds of the Common External Tariff (see the chapter entitled 'Customs Union and Economic Union in the EEC'). Under the current system, the Council of Ministers fixes the size of the Community budget each year, and the total is divided among the member countries according to a scale laid down in the Treaties: 28 per cent each from France, Germany, and Italy; 7·9 per cent each from Belgium and the Netherlands; and 0·2 per cent from Luxembourg. In addition to its administrative budget, Euratom has a research budget fixed at $432 million for the five-year period 1963–7. In the first five years of its existence, Euratom had a research budget of $215 million.

THE MERGER OF THE COMMUNITIES

The logic of gradually increasing economic integration in the European Community has made the eventual fusion of the three existing Communities inevitable. To a growing extent, the process of creating a single economic unit in place of the six national economies of the member countries has been made more difficult by the functional division between the three Communities. The development of a common energy policy, for example, has not been facilitated, in spite of close cooperation between the three Executives, by the fact that coal policy is currently the responsibility of ECSC, oil and natural gas policy the responsibility of EEC, and nuclear-energy policy that of Euratom. Similarly, in the field of transport policy, the ECSC High Authority has wide powers of control over the movement of coal and steel products within the Community, but other transport matters are the concern of the Common Market Commission.

A treaty merging the three Community Executives into a single Commission of the European Communities, and creating a single Council of Ministers for all three Communities, was in fact signed by the member governments on 8 April 1965. It was due to come into force on 1 January 1966, but as a result of the political crisis which developed in the Community in mid-1965, has not yet been implemented. This treaty covers only the fusion of policy-making and administrative institutions of the Communities, and for an interim period the single Executive and the single Council of Ministers continue to implement the three separate Community Treaties.

One of the main tasks of the single Executive after the merger treaty has been implemented, however, will be to put forward proposals for a single Community treaty to replace the Paris Treaty and the two Rome Treaties. Only when a single European Community Treaty comes into effect will it be legally correct to speak of 'the European Community', rather than 'the European Communities'. The other major task which will face the merged Executive as soon as it takes office will be to supervise the integration of the currently separate staffs of the three existing Communities.

The Executive merger treaty stipulated that the single Community Executive would have fourteen members initially, but that this number would be reduced to nine when a single Community treaty came into effect, or within three years at the most. In the discussions which led up to the merger treaty, it was agreed by the member governments that the new Community Executive would have its headquarters in Brussels, and that Luxembourg would be compensated for the loss of the ECSC High Authority by becoming, in principle, the headquarters of all or most of the Community's legal and financial bodies.

BIBLIOGRAPHY

Bebr, Gerhard. *Judicial Control of the European Communities*, Stevens, London; Frederick A. Praeger, New York, 1962.

Brierley, Caroline. *The Making of European Policy*, Oxford Univ. Press, London, 1961; New York, paperback ed. 1963.

Deniau, Jean F. *The Common Market*, Barrie and Rockliff/Pall Mall Press, London; Frederick A. Praeger, New York, 3rd ed. 1963.

Forsyth, Murray. *The Parliament of the European Communities*, Political and Economic Planning, London, 1964.

Hallstein, Walter. *United Europe: Challenge and Opportunity*, Harvard Univ. Press, Cambridge, Mass.; Oxford Univ. Press, London, 1962.

Henderson, W. O. *The Genesis of the Common Market*, Frank Cass, London, 1962; Quadrangle, Chicago, Ill., 1963.

Lindberg, Leon N. *The Political Dynamics of European Economic Integration*, Oxford Univ. Press, London; Stanford Univ. Press, Stanford, Calif., 1963.

Lippmann, Walter. *Western Unity and the Common Market*, Little, Brown, Boston, Mass.; Hamish Hamilton, London, 1962.

Mayne, Richard. *The Community of Europe*, Gollancz, London, 1962; W. W. Norton, New York, paperback ed. 1963.

Noel, Emile. *How the EEC's Institutions Work*, Community Topics Series No. 11, European Community Information Service, London, 1963.

Pryce, Roy. *The Political Future of the European Community*, Federal Trust/Marshbank, London 1962.

Weil, Gordon L. (ed.) *A Handbook of the European Community*, Pall Mall Press, London; Frederick A. Praeger, New York, 1965.

European Community Information Service. *A Guide to the Study of the European Community* (bibliography), London, 1965.

Political and Economic Planning. *European Organisations: An Objective Survey*, Allen and Unwin, London, 1959. *Aspects of European Integration*, London, 1962. *Budgetary Control in the European Economic Community*, Occasional Paper No. 6, London, 1964.

CUSTOMS UNION AND ECONOMIC UNION IN THE EEC

ROY PRYCE

ALTHOUGH the Treaty of Rome is a lengthy and complex document it does little more than sketch in the programme of integration on which the six countries of the European Economic Community (EEC) embarked in January 1958. When seven and a half years later, in June 1965, the Community ground to a halt because of a crisis precipitated by the French government, much still remained to be done. Nevertheless in the intervening years, as a result of intensive effort, the member states had progressed far along the path towards a customs union. They had also made substantial progress in laying the foundations—and in some sectors a good deal of the superstructure—of economic union.

THE CUSTOMS UNION

The basis on which the Community rests is provided by a customs union: that is, the abolition of tariffs, quotas and other similar obstacles to the free movement of goods between its members and the substitution of a common external tariff for the separate national tariffs towards countries outside the Community. The mechanism by which these twin objectives are to be reached was laid down in considerable detail in the Rome Treaty. Its application in the period 1958–1965 gave rise to comparatively little difficulty. During 1958 there were fears that the French might not be willing to make the first internal tariff cuts due on 1 January 1959; however, the economic and financial reforms carried out in December 1958 under the Fifth Republic enabled France to respect its obligations. Later on the original timetable was twice speeded up by decisions of the Council of Ministers on 12 May 1960 and 15 May 1962. By 1 January 1966 the total internal tariff cuts amounted to 80 per cent of the levels in force in 1957. All quotas on industrial goods had been abolished by the end of 1961, and quotas on agricultural goods either substantially increased or replaced by levies. (See Common Market Timetable, page 583.)

The greater part of the common external tariff was agreed during the negotiations of the Treaty. Most duties were a mathematical average of existing levels applied by France, Germany, Italy and Benelux (the latter countries already having a common external tariff). The result gave a moderate level of protection, its average incidence being lower than that of either the United Kingdom or the United States. Those items on which no agreement proved possible at this stage—there were 77 headings in this category—were grouped together in 'List G' for subsequent negotiation. These were items like aluminium, zinc, cork, sulphur and vehicle parts on

COMMON MARKET TIMETABLE

(Entries in italics show measures taken under the decisions of 12 May 1960 and 15 May 1962 to speed up the Common Market timetable)

Date	Internal tariff cuts		Quota enlargements (total)	Alignment of national tariffs on common external tariff: reduction of difference (up or down)
	Total	*Minimum for each product*		
STAGE 1 1958	—	—	—	—
1959 1 Jan.	By 10%	By 10%	By 20%	—
1960 1 Jan.	—	—	By 20%	—
1 July	By 10%	By 10%	—	—
31 Dec.	*By 10%*[1]	*By 10%*[1]	—	—
1961 1 Jan.	—	—	By 20%	—
31 Dec.	By 10%	By 10%	Abolition of quota restrictions on industrial goods[2]	*By 30%* (common tariff fully applied where difference amounted to 15% or less)

By end of Stage 1: Total internal tariff cuts on each product amounted to 40%. Export duties had been abolished. This Stage ended on 31 December 1961.

Date	Internal tariff cuts		Quota enlargements (total)	Alignment of national tariffs on common external tariff: reduction of difference (up or down)
STAGE 2 1962 1 July	*By 10%*	*By 10%*	—	—
1963 1 July	By 10%	By 5%	—	*By 30%*
1964 31 Dec.	By 10%	By 5%	—	—
1965 31 Dec.	By 10%	By 5%	—	—

By end of Stage 2: Total internal tariff cuts on each product were at least 65%.

Date	Internal tariff cuts		Quota enlargements (total)	Alignment of national tariffs on common external tariff: reduction of difference (up or down)
STAGE 3 1966 1 Jan.	Acting on the Commission's proposal, the Council fixes the rate of remaining internal tariff cuts during Stage 3		—	—
1969 31 Dec.	To zero	To zero	—	Full adoption of common external tariff

By end of Stage 3: All internal tariffs and quotas, and restrictions on the free movement of men, services and capital, to be removed. This Stage may only be prolonged by unanimous vote of the Council on a proposal by the Commission; the total transition period may not be prolonged by more than three years.

Source: Information Service
of the European Communities.

[1] By 5% only for agricultural products.
[2] Special arrangements were made for enlargement of industrial quotas.

which the interests of the member states were in conflict. But the duties on these items, with the single exception of petroleum products, were settled in a package deal concluded by the Council of Ministers on 2 March 1960.

The Treaty provided that national tariffs should be aligned on the common external tariff in three stages corresponding to the three stages of the transitional period. The first step which reduced the difference between the two levels by 30 per cent was duly taken on 31 December 1961 at the end of the first stage; the second was brought forward to 1 July 1963. The remaining step will be taken on 1 July 1968.

These successive steps have meant some raising of German and Benelux tariffs towards non-Community countries and a corresponding reduction of the higher French and Italian duties. A provisional 20-per-cent reduction in the tariff was however made in 1961, part of which was later consolidated in the 'Dillon round' of tariff negotiations in the GATT (General Agreement on Tariffs and Trade). A further reduction of up to 50 per cent on industrial items is theoretically possible in the event of a successful outcome of the 'Kennedy round' of negotiations in the same body. The difficulties encountered since these negotiations began in 1963 suggest however that the eventual outcome will at best be of much more modest dimensions.

ECONOMIC UNION

In addition to the free movement of goods, integration also implies the free circulation of workers and capital, a lifting of national restrictions on the right of firms to set up in other member countries, and of similar restrictions on services (banking, insurance, and those provided by members of the liberal professions, etc). At the same time it requires the creation of common or harmonised policies in certain sectors and a coordination of general economic, financial and budgetary policy. As the Treaty gives only an outline of the objectives to be reached and the means for their attainment, a very large part of the activity of the Community's institutions has been devoted to these matters, some of which—like agriculture—have proved to be of great complexity and considerable political difficulty.

Neither the free circulation of workers nor that of capital has yet given rise to major problems. With regard to workers the principle introduced by the Treaty is that nationals of the member states should be free to take up offers of jobs anywhere in the Community. This was regarded as of especial importance by the Italians as a way of reducing their heavy structural unemployment at the time the Treaty was negotiated. The trade unions in the other countries were less enthusiastic, fearing that employers might turn to Italians in order to depress wages or resist claims for higher pay and better working conditions. It was therefore decided to introduce free movement in stages.

A first regulation was passed in August 1961 and a second in February 1964. While the first maintained a priority for each national labour market and restricted the right of free movement to those seeking permanent employment, the second abolished this priority and extended free movement to seasonal and frontier workers, at the same time giving migrant workers the right to be joined by all their dependents in the country of their new employment. The effect of these measures has not, however, been very marked. This has been due mainly to the general tightness on the labour market produced by the high level of economic activity which characterised most of the period up to 1966.

In May 1960 the Community unconditionally freed a wide range of capital movements and conditionally freed most other types. Since then the major emphasis has been on harmonising legislative and administrative arrangements which in many cases have proved to be of more material importance than formal prohibitions in obstructing capital movements.

In contrast progress has been much slower with the right of establishment throughout the six member countries and the freeing of services. A general programme was agreed in October 1961 but it was already clear in 1965 that certain important parts of it—notably the coordination of legislative and administrative provisions and the mutual recognition of professional qualifications—would not be completed by the end of the transition period. The main reason for this was the extraordinary complexity of the problems in this sector; a contributory factor the smallness of the staff the EEC Commission had working on them. Completion of the programme will be necessary before full economic union can become a reality, and it has not yet had any major impact on the activities involved.

Common Policies

Agriculture

The formation of a common agricultural policy has been a central concern of the Community and the subject of repeated and major political difficulties. It is only due to the efforts and skill of Sicco Mansholt, the member of the EEC Commission responsible for this sector, that a steady momentum has been maintained in spite of the acute problems of drawing together what were previously six separate and divergent national agricultural policies.

The first major decision was taken in December 1960. The Council then accepted the principle proposed by the Commission of substituting a system of levies on a number of major products for the tariffs and quotas which had previously been used by the member countries to protect their farmers. The levies fulfil a dual purpose. As applied to trade in farm products within the Community they will be progressively reduced until by 31 December 1969 they will disappear to give free trade in these products between the member states. At the same time variable levies at the external frontier of the Community will give permanent protection against fluctuations in world prices, being based on the difference between internal prices (maintained in some cases by support buying and other devices) and world market prices. In January 1962 agreement was reached on detailed marketing arrangements for a series of products after a marathon session during which, as *Time* magazine reported, 'three officials collapsed with heart attacks and stubble-bearded, trigger-tempered delegates fought long into the night, stoked with double whiskies'. The products in question were grains, pigmeat, eggs, poultry, fruit and vegetables, and wine. Other regulations were later approved for beef and veal, rice and dairy products. In each case, however, a decision on the future common price level was left until later.

This was the next major hurdle and one that was successfully surmounted for the key sector of grain prices in December 1964. The German government, under heavy pressure from its own farmers, had resisted the Commission's proposals for a reduction of current German wheat prices to a level close to the average between these and the lower French prices. It gave way, however, in the face of pressure from the other members and in particular a threat from President de Gaulle to withdraw from the Community unless agreement was reached. To compensate for lower producer prices in Germany,

Italy and Luxembourg it was agreed to pay a total of some £150 million to the affected farmers up to the end of the transition period. It was also agreed that the common prices would not be applied until 1 July 1967.

This agreement was typical of a policy which has had to recognise that what is politically possible must take priority over what may be economically desirable. While Mansholt found little difficulty in resisting the more extreme demands of the farmers' organisations—which were in any case divided among themselves on all the major issues—he was well aware that the price of success was a system that would guarantee much the same level of protection as that formerly maintained by national measures. In some cases the degree of protection has increased, though it would seem more by accident than by design. It is however very difficult to assess the extent to which the new marketing arrangements have affected prices. On the whole they seem to have had less immediate effect than more general economic trends, and seasonal and cyclical factors. (While for instance egg prices rose under the impact of the new regime they soon fell again as a result of an increase in production.)

The long-term effects of the policy can only be a matter of speculation. In early 1967 no common price levels had been in force long enough for their effects to be visible. Some of the marketing arrangements for sugar, vegetable oils and fats, for instance, had only recently been agreed. Many other aspects have also to be worked out. Little has yet been done with regard to structural policy or the harmonisation of state aids; nor have any of the authorised producer groups on which the Commission sets much store yet been set up. There are also a number of external factors which may impinge on the practical effects of the common policy. The Commission for instance has proposed a binding of support amounts in the framework of the Kennedy round of GATT negotiations. It has also expressed its willingness to enter into negotiations for international agreements on certain commodities.

At the same time the general pattern of farming in the Community is rapidly changing under the impact of other factors. Since 1958, for instance, the active labour force on the farms has fallen from some 18 millions to under 12 millions, and this flight from the land is expected to continue. (In France, for example, the numbers engaged in agriculture are likely to be halved in the next twenty years.) No other sector of the Community's economy is undergoing such rapid change. But while its agricultural problems may become in the long run politically more manageable they seem certain to provide in the foreseeable future as many explosive problems as they have done since 1958. In the meantime it is a remarkable achievement that the transition to the new policies has been carried out without any disruption, and that the farmers themselves who (with the exception of the Dutch) were initially hostile to integration are now among its more fervent supporters.

Competition

While it was generally recognised by the Treaty-makers that a common policy for agriculture would have to be based on managed marketing, much emphasis was placed on the need in other sectors to ensure a maximum degree of competition. Article 85 of the Treaty prohibits agreements or concerted practices which prevent, restrain or distort competition, such as price-fixing, market-sharing, restriction of production or of technical developments and discriminatory supply conditions, if they are likely to affect trade between the member states. (It does however permit those agreements which contribute to better production or distribution or to technical progress.) Article 86 also declares an abuse of a dominant position as contrary to the Treaty.

Although these provisions were held to be immediately binding on the member states the Community institutions had to work out a common policy to put them into effect. After much discussion a system of compulsory registration of agreements was applied by decision of the Council of Ministers in March 1962. Provision was made for the 'negative clearance' of those types of agreements which the Commission deemed to fall within the permitted categories, but heavy fines were laid down for those firms which persisted in maintaining agreements judged to be incompatible with the Treaty. More than 37,000 agreements were duly registered; not surprisingly the Commission made slow progress in dealing with them. To lighten its load the Council agreed to a number of group exceptions, and the Commission for its part sought to reach decisions on certain other major categories. As a result of its pressure a number of agreements have been dissolved by their authors without a formal decision, and others adjusted to conform with the Treaty. A good deal of pressure has however been applied by industrial circles to persuade the Commission to authorise agreements promoting common action between firms faced by strong competition from outside the Community, in particular from the United States. In 1966 it was still too early to judge how readily the Commission would react to such arguments or how stringent and successful the control of restrictive trade practices would prove to be.

By 1966 the considerable reduction of internal tariffs had revealed the importance of disparities in national legislation and administrative regulations as a factor in distorting competition. The varying incidence of taxation, for instance, became a matter of increasing concern. In November 1962 the Commission put forward a first measure to deal with this problem by proposing the general adoption of an added value tax as the major instrument of indirect taxation. This had still to be agreed in 1966, though much of the initial opposition to it had by then disappeared. At the same time a start was made in the harmonisation of legislation covering other sectors, such as food and drugs and tenders for public contracts. Many trade associations were themselves actively engaged in preparing their own schemes for harmonisation on matters ranging from the hallmarking of precious metals to regulations concerning beauty parlours.

Some perceptible progress has also been made in reducing the discrimination implicit in state-controlled monopolies; a draft convention has been drawn up to harmonise the law with regard to bankruptcy; and another has been prepared on patents. Agreement on the latter, however, was held up by a divergence between the member states on whether an agreement should be limited to members of the Community or should be extended to a wider group of countries, including for instance the United Kingdom (which expressed its wish to be included).

Transport

Progress in the application of a common policy to transport has been slow and the results obtained by 1966 were small. The major reason for this was the much lower priority attached to this sector by governments and the opposition of the Netherlands to the adoption of a less liberal system than their own, and one which might consequently reduce the work for their transport concerns. ('The Dutch think they are God's own carriers' commented one exasperated official after another abortive meeting.) The first major decisions were not taken until June 1965 and these provided only a framework within which detailed regulations were to be worked out in two stages, the first to stretch between 1966 and December 1969; the second up to the end of 1972. Fork rates (compulsory maximum and minimum rates between which the charges have to fall) were to be introduced for cross-frontier road and rail transport, while water transport concerns were to be required only to publish rates lying outside the limits of non-compulsory rate brackets.

Commercial policy

It is quite clear that the member states of the Community will sooner or later need to arrive at a common commercial policy and the Treaty provision (Article 111) speaks of bringing it about not later than the end of the transition period. Although the member states have had to adopt a common position with regard to a series of requests for trade agreements by other countries, including Israel, Iran and the Lebanon, and to the tariff negotiations in GATT, progress in other respects has been slow. In 1964 the commission proposed a new series of measures pointing out the urgency in particular of common action with regard to trade with countries of the Eastern bloc, and low-wage countries. Some progress has been made in adopting uniform lists of quota-free products, in harmonising insurance and Credit schemes to aid exports, and in joint consultation before the conclusion of bilateral trade agreements. But in other important respects—for instance, the harmonisation of export aids, anti-dumping measures and quotas—much remains to be done.

Social policy

One of the weakest aspects of the Treaty, social policy remains for the most part firmly in the hands of national governments. The French and Germans in particular have strongly resisted attempts by the Commission to extend the range of social harmonisation specifically sanctioned by the Treaty. Such provisions as were inserted in it owe their origin mainly to French fears that their own manufacturing costs were higher than those of other member countries because of higher social charges. It was this for instance which lay behind the obligation to introduce equal pay for men and women by the end of the first stage of the transition period. Formally this obligation has been respected though its application in practice is far from complete. The social fund, from which national governments are repaid half the cost of re-training schemes, has also been of limited significance because of the narrowness of its terms of reference. The trade unions in the Community have become increasingly restive with the lack of progress in the social field.

Economic and financial policy

As integration has advanced it has become evident that a successful economic union can only function if the member states coordinate their general economic policies to a degree that was not envisaged in the Treaty. As however these policies belong to a very sensitive area of national sovereignty the Community has proceeded with great caution in this direction. An early development was the creation in 1960 of a Trade Cycle Policy Committee consisting of senior national officials and the Commission which, on the basis of annual and quarterly reports by the latter, has sought, with

49

moderate success, to prevent the development of imbalances within the Community's economy. In the meantime the Monetary Committee has also provided a forum for the comparison of national policies and discussion of trends and problems in this crucial sector. The finance ministers of the member states have also met regularly for a similar purpose. In 1964 at the suggestion of the Commission a new series of steps was taken to intensify these exchanges. The terms of reference of the Monetary Committee were extended to include prior consultation on important issues of international monetary policy, and a new committee composed of governors of the central banks of the Community (Deutsche Bundesbank, Banque de France, etc) was established. A Budgetary Policy Committee of senior officials was also set up with the aim of a gradual coordination in this sector.

At the same time there were other important developments. In April 1964 the Council for the first time issued, on the basis of a proposal from the Commission, a recommendation to the member states aimed at correcting what it considered to be dangerously inflationary tendencies, especially in Germany and Italy. This, in brief, suggested the pursuit of a liberal import policy; the maintenance or imposition of credit restrictions; and tight control over public expenditure, with additional taxation to cover any increased deficit. This recommendation was more important as a sign of the increasing impact of integration than in its direct effects, though it occasioned a good deal of controversy in Italy where the socialists in the centre left government resented external pressure to pursue a deflationary policy.

Italy, however, stood to gain a good deal from efforts the Commission was also making to persuade the member governments to adopt a common approach to regional policy. In December 1961 three working parties were set up to study ways of dealing with underdeveloped regions in the Community, those faced by a decline in traditional industries, and the problems of inducing firms to set up in such areas. On the basis of these reports, which were published in July 1964, the Commission worked out a first memorandum on regional policy which it presented to the Council in May 1965. It suggested that regional development programmes be worked out with a high priority given to schemes for the retraining of the local work force. In the meantime substantial aid from the European Investment Bank had been made available for the industrial development of southern Italy, the Community contributing in particular to the financing of a major new steel works at Taranto.

An even more significant development in 1964 was the creation of a Medium-Term Economic Policy Committee under the chairmanship of Dr Wolfram Langer, German secretary of state for economic affairs. The task it was given, to quote the Commission, was 'the establishment of overall medium-term economic forecasts in order to clarify decisions on economic policy'. In effect it began to work out an economic programme for the Community for the period up to 1970. Its agenda included an examination of the choices to be made in terms of basic objectives, the conditions of economic growth, ways of securing the harmonious development of the various factors of production (including professional training schemes, competition policy, investment policy, and scientific research programmes), and what would be required in terms of action by member states with regard to public expenditure and taxation. This was an exercise in indicative planning which at one stage seemed likely to have profound consequences on many areas of both national and Community policy-making. A five-year economic programme was published in April 1966. The crisis of June 1965, however, had slowed down the Committee's work.

THE CRISIS OF JUNE 1965

The occasion of the crisis was a package proposal put forward by the Commission which linked the future arrangements for financing the common agricultural policy both with measures to create an autonomous budget for the Community (out of the proceeds of the levies on imports of food and the duties derived from the common tariff) and an extension of the budgetary powers of the European Parliament. The immediate break occurred over the unwillingness of some member states (notably Italy) to commit themselves to a definite settlement of the problem of financing the common farm policy, on which France insisted. Behind this conflict lay a series of deeper issues touching on the willingness of the member states to accept the further merging of sovereignty implied by the other aspects of the Commission's package and also by the requirement in the Treaty that in the third stage of the transition period (reached at the end of 1965) weighted majority voting should be introduced for most major issues. In his press conference of September 1965 President de Gaulle made it clear that he was unwilling to accept this and that he was also determined to curb the powers of the Commission. In the meantime France had ceased to take part in meetings of the Council and had thus brought the Community to a standstill.

It was nevertheless significant that the French did not go further: the Community was consigned to the deep freeze but not to the scrap heap. Their own freedom of manoeuvre was limited by the fact that although economic union was far from completed, business circles had come not only to accept the programme of integration but also to rely on its fulfilment. Attitudes had been readjusted to the new dimensions of a common market; so too had investment and marketing policies. Moreover, more than 300 Community professional organisations throughout the Six, representing industrial trade associations, farmers' unions, trade unions, commercial, transport and other interests, had been set up to concert policy and take common action. By their own action they had extended the processes of integration even beyond the wide bounds of the formal Community system, and had also acted very often to obtain the more rapid completion of the programme laid down in the Treaties. Many of them now protested against the French action: for them a reversion to a purely national economic framework was unthinkable.

These developments combined with the firm front maintained by the other five member states during the crisis eventually led to a compromise at a meeting of the Council of Ministers in Luxembourg at the end of January 1966. The Six agreed to disagree about the use of weighted majority voting, France insisting on the continued need for unanimity; they also agreed on minor changes in the relationship between the Commission and the Council, and on a programme of work for the coming months. France then agreed to resume active membership of the Community. The basic political divergences between France and her partners had not, however, been resolved. Though impelled forward by the economic expectations engendered by its early success, the EEC seemed certain to encounter more rough weather as it neared the end of its transition period.

FROM ECONOMIC UNION
TO POLITICAL UNION

PIERRE URI

THE aims of the European Communities have always been political. Does this mean that the Communities will lead to a political union between the member countries?

GROWTH OF THE EUROPEAN COMMUNITIES

Integration started with the pooling of coal and steel, which might seem a strange way to begin, for the freeing of trade in two isolated products for any length of time must cause serious economic distortion. It was a novel approach, which has, however, proved successful: by creating an unbalanced situation the member countries forced themselves to go a step further in order to restore the balance. Criticism gave a new impetus to the whole operation, by involving the critics in the business of European integration.

Coal and steel both had a symbolic value. Coal was still the main source of power for the manufacturing industries, and steel was, and still is, the mainstay of the armaments industry; together therefore they played a decisive part in peace and war. But above all they provided an opportunity to set up a new kind of institution to administer common interests. This fundamental urge is reflected in the Schuman declaration,[1] part of which is incorporated in the preamble to the Paris (or European Coal and Steel Community) Treaty, which speaks of putting an end to centuries of warfare and bloodshed and laying the foundations of institutions to guide the common destiny of the member states.

It soon became clear that the idea of a body representing the Community as a whole, which would conduct a sort of dialogue with the member states, was an important one, and could be extended to other spheres. It was next taken up in the project for a European Defence Community (EDC). This project was first conceived at the time of the negotiations on the Schuman plan. The basic aim was not only to enable France and Germany to be reconciled, but to settle the status of Germany, then still in the hands of the Allied High Commission, by direct transition from an occupation regime to a new European system under which Germany would be integrated into a much larger entity. The United States, alarmed by the threats to Western

[1] See 'The Structure of the European Community', p. 570.

Europe from outside, proposed the reconstruction of a German army of twelve divisions to strengthen the defence forces of the West. The danger of building up an independent German army and high command, and the blatant contradiction between reestablishing a national force and the attempts at creating a supranational organisation (represented by the European Coal and Steel Community), required an immediate counter-proposal. In retrospect the EDC, the resulting project, was clearly inopportune. Not only was national opinion probably not ready for it, but for years afterwards one member of the Community at least (France) was engaged in wars outside Europe, and 'exceptional' withdrawals from the proposed integrated force would have been more often the rule than integration. The draft itself, which was copied somewhat unimaginatively from the Paris Treaty, had several drawbacks. Although putting great emphasis on the supranational principle, embodied in a nine-member Commissariat, it prevented the Commissariat from working because most of the decisions needed the unanimous agreement of the member states. As the common budget was simply the sum of the defence budgets voted by the national parliaments there was also a danger of insufficient money, since the member countries would have vied with each other to keep their contributions relatively speaking as low as possible.

The difficulty of establishing common forces without a common foreign policy was, however, realised at the time, for without such a policy there could be no decision to use force. Hence the idea of a political community to complement the defence community. The European Assembly's plan to meet this need is not without historical interest, even though it was abandoned when the EDC was rejected by the French parliament. The general structural pattern of an assembly, council of ministers, court of appeal and executive, was copied straight from the Paris Treaty, but this time the executive was to be elected by the assembly. The powers of the executive were essentially the same as those of the High Authority of the Coal and Steel Community (ECSC). As far as diplomacy was concerned, it could only give advice or suggestions, and though there was a chapter devoted to European laws it gave no indication of their content.

The EDC project thus failed to grasp the basic principle to which the European Communities owe their success: the direct relationship between the structure of the institutions and their purpose.

But the structure of the ECSC itself is out of proportion to the work it has to do, as it consists of an executive, an assembly, a consultative committee, a court and a council, to serve only two industries. This is because the intention was to create not simply a model for the future but a framework into which other economic sectors and other spheres still under national control would ultimately be fitted as their time for integration into the European system arrived. Considerable powers had to be delegated to the ECSC from the start, owing to the nature of the two industries: in the coal industry inflexibility of output meeting fluctuating demand, fiercer competition from other kinds of energy, social problems, and the very narrow margin between shortage and surplus; in the steel industry, violent fluctuations in demand depending on the rate of general investment and exports, accompanied by constantly rising costs. At the same time both industries were faced with the need for new large-scale investment, involving considerable time-lag before results could appear, and for long-term investment planning in spite of rapidly changing economic conditions. Thus it was not simply a matter of delegating enough authority to pass temporary measures and to unify the different markets; a sort of economic government was required to deal with so large a variety of problems. The dramatic emergence of the Common Market, after the Rome Treaty was successfully drawn up five years later (1957), showed that this approach and this type of institution were accepted as sound; indeed, the new Community extended the range of its institutions to take in the whole of the economy.

The objectives of this treaty were again political. Whatever the real reasons had been for France's refusal to ratify the EDC Treaty, it looked at the time (1954) like failure for the idea of a united Europe. In fact, the project was rejected because of the hesitations of the French foreign minister, Georges Bidault, in spite of his then being a supporter of the European movement, and because the prime minister, Pierre Mendès-France, was anxious to settle the matter rapidly, since it was seriously dividing the country. Owing largely to a misunderstanding between him and the other NATO governments, Mendès-France decided against the project, with the result that the whole European defence project was defeated inside France by a combination of those who did not wish to give up a French national army and those who were opposed to German rearmament under any circumstances.

After this setback, the question arose how to start moving again. Most of the discussions took place in and around the High Authority of the ECSC in Luxembourg. There were, for instance, cautious suggestions that the High Authority's powers should be widened to include transport and other forms of energy (apart from coal). But it was difficult to justify this when the other industries, to which energy and transport are related, were to remain under separate economic systems; moreover, oil was an international product (coming from outside the Community) and transport, electricity and gas were service industries, so that the High Authority's experience with coal and steel would be of little use, and the difficulties would be out of all proportion to the results desired.

Jean Monnet and Louis Armand came forward with the idea of pooling atomic energy. The fundamental importance of atomic energy for the future and the vast amount of research involved commended the idea, but above all the fact that atomic energy had hitherto had largely military associations meant that the idea appealed strongly to the public. Even so, the governments still had to agree. In one way Euratom was a continuation of one of the main purposes of the Schuman plan: to establish common bases for economic development. The other main purpose was to conduct another experiment in integration in a limited sector, which would then gradually lead to general integration. It is not generally known that the idea of combining these two purposes and establishing a common market for the whole of the economy was a kind of by-product of Euratom. The broader approach was a condition imposed by Germany for accepting an atomic energy community, for Germany did not stand to gain much in this field from an association with the other ECSC members, if integration were not extended to include other economic sectors. Conversely it was the attraction of Euratom which made the French political leaders accept the idea of the Common Market. Whatever the initial attitudes, however, it was not long before the general Common Market became the more important development, on which all the other proposals, concerning energy, transport or the establishment of Euratom, depended. Once again economics and politics came together, while the close relationship between institutional structure and aims was made particularly clear in the new Treaty's plans for an economic union which would go well beyond the scope of a customs union or free trade area.

POLITICAL QUESTIONS IN ECONOMIC TERMS

Customs union and economic union

It is not easy to determine exactly where a 'customs union' ends and 'economic union' begins, for the two concepts can be defined in several ways. One definition is that a customs union concerns only the free movement of goods within a given area, and a common tariff at the border; thus according to this definition, any measure which does not strictly concern goods comes under the definition of economic union. This means not only measures such as free movement of labour and capital, but also common rules of competition applying to business concerns or governments, and, of course, common financial resources and common policies.

A narrower definition of economic union is that it requires constructive action as opposed to the mere removal of obstacles to trade; according to this definition the mere abolition of restrictions of the free movement of capital and labour from one country to the next comes into the same category as measures relating to goods, i.e. a customs union. (This is the position held by some socialists, who regard any free trade measure as being 'right-wing', and who therefore, when the dismantling of tariffs was achieved ahead of schedule in the Common Market, criticised the lack of progress in the creation of common organisations and harmonisation of economic conditions to which the left traditionally attaches importance.)

There is a third possible distinction between a customs union and economic union if the rules of competition, particularly the prohibition of cartels, are considered as an inseparable corollary of free trade. An example of this distinction may be found in EFTA, which is not an economic union but which, according to the Stockholm Convention, has a few basic rules governing competition; on the other hand, it is not concerned with agriculture and there is no common external tariff, both of which are covered by the Rome Treaty.

The problems involved in agriculture, transport and foreign affairs, however, cannot easily be classified under any of these definitions of either customs union or economic union. For example, the movement of goods can involve agriculture only if there is a general agricultural policy and marketing system; any rules for transport will involve rules governing transport prices; and a common external tariff rapidly creates the need for a common trade policy, an aspect, in its turn, of foreign policy. In other words, in order to work these largely divergent elements into a coherent whole, an overall plan is essential: there must be an automatic process by which the plan is implemented, leading to the same close interrelation of parts as obtains in an internal or national market. The more the governments are actively involved in the workings of the economy, in order to ensure expansion, stability, full employment and fair distribution of wealth, the more they will be bound to undertake in common, if they are also to establish a common market between their states.

Harmonisation and coordination

A question which then arises is how far to take joint action in any given sector. In this connection, 'harmonisation' and 'coordination' are terms which are used frequently and generally treated as synonymous, but it may be useful to define them more precisely. The difference between them (whether it be in connection with tax legislation or monetary policy or anything else) can be demonstrated by their relation to an absolute term: complete unification (of states).

In the absence of such unification, harmonisation aims at preventing distortions in competition. Where, for instance, profits taxes differ from one country to another, capital tends to be deflected from economically productive projects into investment on which taxation is less heavy. In a common market concerted action also has to be taken if competition threatens to bring about harmonisation in an undesirable way. For instance, if member countries compete with each other to have the lowest profits taxes, this would inevitably lead to increases in other kinds of taxation. This line of argument led to the insertion into the Treaties of rules to establish equal pay for men and women and standard working hours to govern the application of 'overtime' rates.

Coordination, on the other hand, does not imply the application of permanent rules. Coordination concerns policies, whether they be policies to deal with the immediate economic situation, or longer-term programmes. It does not normally mean that all member countries act in the same way. Instead they often need to act differently, but to complement each other: rates of interest, for example, may be made to vary from one country to the next according to the balance of payments position; and coordination of regional policy means granting aid to some areas and no aid to others in order to avoid a further concentration of industry in the traditional areas. A recent example of coordination in the European Community may be seen in the medium-term programmes which were drawn up jointly as a compromise between countries which have large-scale economic planning and those which do not. These programmes enable the former to base their planning on information concerning a much wider economic area instead of limiting themselves to an isolated view of their national economies. They also force those countries which, like Germany, traditionally avoid using a systematic approach to government programmes, to take all of them together—be it town-planning, transport, education or defence—enabling them to be carried out far more successfully, precisely because each item is no longer considered in isolation.

Of course, it will always be hard to agree to what extent actions should be based on joint decisions, in the interests of a smoothly operating market or a closer-knit Community. Answers to questions such as how much disparity in taxation systems can be allowed without causing damage to the Common Market; how much autonomy is permissible in trade policy to enable each country to pursue its own foreign policy; which industrial and commercial agreements have a purely local significance and which affect the Common Market as a whole; how much disparity in company law can be allowed between one country and the next—answers to all these questions will depend on individual assessments.

The best and most comprehensive solutions require a much more radical approach. For instance, differing systems of indirect taxation are not incompatible with the Common Market provided goods carry the taxes of the country of destination. But if this means that exports to another country (even within the Community) are always exempt from tax, and equalisation taxes are levied on imports, then fiscal frontiers will always remain, which in practice leads to the same kinds of control that are exercised at customs frontiers today. Leaving aside the question of the effects of these taxes on investment, the standardisation of indirect taxation throughout the Community may, therefore, be prompted more by psychological reasons than by strictly economic ones. On the other hand, as the plans for a Common Market added-value tax show, the opportunity for discussion and comparison which standardisation provides leads to schemes which are far sounder economically than many existing national systems which reflect bad habits and outdated traditions.

It always takes time to come to grips with the real, as opposed to the apparent, problems of integration. The absence of European company law or a European type of company has not prevented the existence of a common market nor the formation of joint subsidiaries by companies of different nationalities; the subsidiary companies take the form and abide by the laws of the country in which they are set up. However, the absence of European company law makes mergers between companies of different nationalities practically impossible, with the result that American companies have found it much easier than European ones to reap the benefits of the wider economic area created by the Common Market. This influx of direct foreign investment has made European businessmen realise the need, if not to standardise commercial law and the different types of company, at least to provide alongside existing systems the alternative of a new type of company with a European base.

THE POWERS OF THE COMMUNITY INSTITUTIONS

Logical necessity does not, however, automatically become political reality. In the history of the Community there have been times when progress, instead of being the result of effective and systematic action by the European Institutions, as was intended and hoped by the authors of the Treaties, was rather at the mercy of whim or the interplay of force, cunning and bargaining between the governments.

The Schuman Plan was based on the new concept of supranationalism. A myth such as this had to be created to arouse public opinion in countries which had long been kept apart and opposed to each other. In the Paris Treaty the emphasis is on the powers invested in the High Authority, though almost any decision, apart from the application of the rules of competition, financing the Community and implementing transitional measures, requires the unanimous approval of the Council. The tone is different in the Rome Treaty. It is written in more modest terms. There is a Commission which, for questions other than those connected with the implementation of the Treaty, puts proposals to the Council of Ministers, and it is the Council which takes the decisions. It looks at first sight as if the concept of supranationalism had declined in importance from the Paris Treaty to the Rome Treaty, from the European Coal and Steel Community to the European Common Market and Euratom. On closer examination, however, one finds that this power of proposal has given the later institutions even wider powers than the High Authority possesses: this is illustrated by the fact that there are hardly any matters over which majority decisions are not ultimately possible, provided they are based on a proposal from the Commission.

The Executive—the Commission in one case and the High Authority in the other—is of course not the only body to have a common responsibility towards all six countries jointly. The European Parliament which controls the Executive, and the Community's Court of Justice which settles disputes, are not simply groups of delegates from the different countries; they too have to define a Community viewpoint. The Parliament has indeed followed this pattern, for its members have grouped themselves according to political view, and not according to country or origin. Even the Council of Ministers has a kind of two-way allegiance: it must not only reconcile the interests of the different governments, but must play its part in establishing a policy for the Community as a whole.

This problem of finding the best method of reaching a collective decision affecting several countries at once is an extremely difficult one today. It presents a kind of dilemma: unanimity seems justified because each national government is responsible for certain interests—each has its own work to do and is answerable to parliament and nation—but unanimity may rule out the possibility of common decisions entirely, because the power of veto creates a potential deadlock. Some institutions, such as the Organisation for European Economic Cooperation, have worked satisfactorily under this system. However, the OEEC's important decisions were taken largely under pressure from the Americans; its main function was to administer the funds and operate the Marshall Plan. Some memorable instances on the other hand of the adverse effect of the veto and the unanimity rule can be seen in the history of the United Nations Security Council.

Should the Community then adopt a majority system immediately, for surely majority rule is the very foundation of democracy? The analogy is false, for a majority vote between governments is not the same as a majority decision within a country. All the people making up a nation have the same loyalty or responsibility to their country, even though they may hold different opinions. But governments are responsible for various interests and have pledged themselves to differing causes, and they are bound to act in what they consider to be the interests of their country. Thus a majority vote between governments is far from being an objective decision in the sense that it is within an individual country. It provides a risk of coalitions or of underhand bargaining: some member countries may join hands to obtain decisions at the expense of a minority, or there may be compromises by which votes are bought by concessions which have no bearing on the issues at stake. Neither a system of 'one-country-one-vote', as in the United Nations, nor one of weighted voting based on contributions, as in the International Monetary Fund, has proved really satisfactory.

The European Common Market, with its common authoritative body (the Council of Ministers), its rules of procedure laid down in the Rome Treaty, and its institution (the Commission) for carrying out the decisions of this body by means of discussion and control, is the most original solution yet put forward to solve the problem. The Community does not simply ignore national attitudes, psychological differences and divergent interests; it provides a strictly realistic solution in order to counter the divergences in the initial outlook and circumstances of the countries concerned; a group of men—the Commission—have been appointed to think out and propose new formulae, to create a balanced approach and to provide a concrete idea of the common interest. Supranationalism and cooperation between countries are therefore not contradictory terms in the Community system. It is based on cooperation, but cooperation better organised and made more effective because a body of men can stimulate the parties involved into joint action.

Majority rule

The Common Market has solved the dilemma that unanimity leads to deadlock, and majority voting to coalitions or bartering, by providing a method by which a genuine majority rule can be achieved. Two aspects should be emphasised. First there is the transition period. The Rome Treaty stipulates that the unanimity rule will operate for a period which varies in length according to the type of problem, and it is only after this period has expired that majority voting becomes the rule—except for certain types of decision for which it was not possible to lay down a time-table in advance. This means that member countries are encouraged to reach an agreement unanimously, and to make the necessary concessions before the time for a decisive vote comes, from which a country might lose even more. The other aspect of procedure is still more important: it is to ensure that, except in very rare and insignificant cases, majority votes by the Council are never taken *in vacuo*; they must be taken on the basis of a proposal coming from an independent body, the Commission. Therefore supranationalism in the Community, if we can still give it that name, by no means involves the loss of sovereignty, and does not mean that a country has to throw itself at the mercy of its co-members without guarantee that a common interest is being served.

The ingenious mechanism which was devised to ensure this—that majority decisions can be taken only on a proposal put forward by the Commission, and that these proposals can be altered only by unanimous agreement in the Council—has led to a dialogue between the parties concerned. There is little chance of unanimous agreement against the Commission, and it is not possible for a majority of countries to force the Commission's hand. Should the Commission consent to a majority vote which ran counter to the rightful interests of the member countries or of the Community as a whole, it would be censured by the Assembly or have its decision nullified by the Court. On the other hand, there is nothing to prevent it from continually adjusting its proposals until they are acceptable to the Council.

It is not surprising that the criticisms levelled against the system by France have not been taken up by the other Common Market countries. First, it is not true that the majority voting rule only came into force effectively with the third stage of the transition period: it was simply widened then to include a large number of decisions affecting agriculture and transport; it had already been applied without any particular difficulty in a considerable number of other spheres. Moreover, in practice, majority votes are fairly rare; they facilitate agreement instead of leading to deadlock, for the fact that it is possible to use a majority vote often makes it unnecessary to do so. (Votes have been weighted in a very simple way, using the figures 1, 2 and 4 to ensure that no country alone has the power of veto—not even the three Benelux countries together, for their combined population and output do not amount to half that of one of the three larger member countries.)

The French government has maintained, further, that the move to a majority vote (for decisions on agriculture) would enable other countries to take back the concessions they had made under the unanimous voting system. This is a surprising attitude to adopt, and quite contrary to general principles of law, since the decisions have been taken for a definite period of time and can normally be changed only by the same procedure as that by which they were taken. By criticising both the fact that the Community's institutions have been given certain powers, and the fact that majority voting has been made possible, the French government has contradicted itself and wilfully ignored the whole point of the Community system: the indissoluble link between majority voting by governments in the Council and proposals issued by an independent body (the Commission). Obviously the Commission would not want simply to abandon its responsibilities for agriculture, nor could the Council take these responsibilities away, unless the Commission itself proposed such a move.

The crisis which began in June 1965[1] was only overcome eight months later in Luxembourg by acknowledging the differences between France and her partners. France is against any extension of the majority voting rule and has stated that it will block any decision in which another country is put in the minority, by uniting with it. The other countries uphold the majority principle and will not give way on it. France, however, has reserved the right to resume its boycott if it does not agree with any particular decision. An unkind summary of the way the dispute was settled—or, if one prefers, papered over—could be made as follows: France is the only one of the member countries which is likely to find itself in the minority, but if this occurs, it reserves the right to break its Treaty obligations.

In all probability the whole system will continue to function in spite of the shock it has received. The vital problem then will be whether the Community institutions can be made to develop gradually and continuously into the institutions needed for a united Europe, and whether economic union may become political union.

THE NATURE OF POLITICAL UNION

There is much ambiguity concerning the extent to which a problem or a decision is political. In a sense everything which the Communities have achieved so far is political, not so much in the achievements of the institutions themselves, where the political content is obvious, but in the sectors of the economy which have been reorganised or given a new framework. To begin with, everything concerning agriculture—production, guidance, maintenance of farm income, the decrease in the farming population—is implicitly political, in the sense that these questions directly affect the electorate. Fiscal reforms, such as the harmonisation of the tax systems in the different member countries, are also essentially political measures because the distribution of revenue and economic power between different sections of the population will be deeply affected by them. All this is political also in that the Community's activities have not been based on logic alone but have affected and involved a whole range of national customs, feelings, pressures and arrangements. 'When we are agreed', one international civil servant has said, 'a problem is economic; when we do not agree then it is political'. There is considerable truth in this, for sometimes a problem can be settled by exact calculation, and at other times a wide range of imponderable elements have also to be taken into account.

Economic problems also of course become political problems the more closely they are related to the general aims and policies of a country. This explains the tension between international agreements and national resistance to their application. Financial policy, credit policy and incomes policy all make up monetary policy, the aim of which is to ensure overall stability, fair distribution of wealth and expansion. This is obviously an essential part of government action. Similarly, in foreign trade the Community will inevitably move from a common external tariff to a common trade policy. Simple international trade agreements have for some time now provided for less important products to make up the trade balance between the countries concerned, and generally speaking this form of arrangement no longer leads to internal political difficulties for the governments concerned.

---

[1] France withdrew from the Council of Ministers as a result of a disagreement with the other five member countries over the arrangements for agriculture in the Community.

A common trade policy will, however, involve a great many other highly political decisions; for instance, whether to trade with China, or with all, or some, of the East European countries; it will involve taking sides in the Arab–Israel dispute or even trying to bring the two together; it will involve a joint decision on whether to open up the European market to the developing countries instead of pursuing a self-contradictory and ineffective policy of aid without trade for these countries; it will also mean recognising the differences between Africa, South-East Asia and Latin America. So that in concrete terms, a common trade policy, if it is ever launched, would have a very strong bearing on more than two-thirds of the basic foreign policy problems of most of the member countries.

Apart from the irrationality of the 'package' nature of decisions on questions like agriculture, financial or commercial policy—questions which ought in fact to involve as highly logical and scientific an approach as possible—there are some matters in which valid political aims are completely at variance and at times even in contradiction with economic good sense: for instance, the question of associating the Community with one or other of the Mediterranean European countries, for which, practically speaking, the Community gets nothing but bills; or, of course, all so-called problems of prestige. And lastly, there are issues which by their very nature cannot be subjected to the kind of approach the Community uses because they are based on a different set of values, whether valid or not: these are diplomacy and defence, the decisions which affect the continuing existence of the member states as such and determine decisions of peace or war.

There are two basic difficulties before the Community in moving from economic to political union. First is the question of method. In the economic sphere it has been possible to introduce changes gradually so that their effects are not too severe, and by progressively increasing the number of joint decisions to soften the impact of the Community on national institutions. In diplomacy and defence, however, there seems to be a barrier which has to be broken: it involves the abandonment of all that is fundamental to the separate existence of the national governments, which fear to find themselves reduced overnight to being part of a federation, deprived of international status and with no more autonomy than provinces. The second, and more important difficulty, is that it is not easy for the peoples of the member countries to abandon their traditional national outlooks, which are often different from and even opposed to those of the other members, and accept common objectives. The difficulty is even greater when diplomacy becomes an end in itself, when a country's foreign policy consists essentially of being noticed rather than contributing to the creation of a more ordered and less unjust world.

Before answers to these difficulties can be found two points must be clearly understood. First, there are some problems such as frontiers, or relations with former colonies or overseas possessions, which are essentially national problems. No country will want to act on the advice of the others when dealing with these, still less hand over decisions on them to others. The only point in discussing them is for consultation or information. The logical line of approach would indeed be, for a country which is going its own way in these fields, to cease expecting to have the full support of the others in the name of solidarity. Most of these questions have been inherited from the past; some of them have already been settled and others may disappear as time goes on. For these purely national problems there should be a kind of transition period until they have all been solved.

The second point is that in spite of flashes in the pan, for countries as small as those of Western Europe independent foreign policies can only be illusory, unless aims are negative. These countries can independently play a destructive role, refuse to cooperate or break up common institutions, but beyond that all they can do is to strike attitudes or play games. None of them has achieved a special relationship with China, Latin America or the Soviet Union, and indeed they can have no real influence on world affairs except by joining their efforts in some common approach, since alone they have too little to offer.

Joint political action

Critics of the Community say that political action must be backed by national feelings, on behalf of which sacrifices can be demanded and made. There is, however, no real disagreement about the fundamental requirements of politics, and no one has ever maintained that anything can be achieved by setting up a disembodied technocracy. Nor has anyone imagined that nations can be merged together immediately, or a European nation born overnight which will command the same affection and loyalty as the traditional other country. On the contrary, it is as a result of clearly recognising the difficulties that will have to be overcome that a body has been created which aims gradually to replace opposing passions with common objectives. There is an inherent contradiction in the view that political action can be defined as action for which men are prepared to die, and in the sketch of political union, put forward by its supporters, which limits such a union to periodical meetings of heads of state or government, on the grounds that new nations cannot be founded. Take the most typical example of this contradiction in action: the decision to use atomic weapons. It is just possible to conceive of a nation deciding to use them, but in doing so it risks destroying itself; it is even harder to conceive of a collective decision by several countries, but this is the only kind of decision which would offer them some chance of avoiding disaster. Thus an administrative arrangement of periodical meetings between heads of state would be hopelessly weak in the face of the urgent and dramatic decisions which they might have to take.

The question remains whether the existing system of Community institutions can be extended as it stands into the political sphere. One essential prelude to this (though by itself it would not be enough) would be the formation of an independent body to make proposals on long-term European aims, and to instigate concerted action in times of crisis. As far as the procedure for holding meetings is concerned, there is of course a great difference between meetings held at a fixed date between governments and meetings called by a commission to discuss specific proposals worked out in advance. The first, as the history of the Franco-German Treaty of 1963 has shown, is quite likely to achieve nothing except to bring into the open, and possibly aggravate, disagreements. But meetings arranged to work out a policy, or called to deal with specific emergencies, provide an impetus of their own and their importance can be adjusted according to the importance of the issues at stake—as the history of the Common Market has shown.

This could not be the final answer, however. Political union is too specific a problem to be solved by preconceived plans. The answer cannot be given in the abstract. European integration since the second world war has been a success because instead of following an abstract scheme, it proceeded by sudden bounds. It began by an agreement on coal and steel, and the logical thing would have been to extend integration to other industrial sectors.

Circumstances led instead to the projected Defence Community, but when this failed the scene of action switched suddenly to general economic integration. The use of a variety of approaches is the key to success.

If the political aims of European integration are to be achieved it must be understood that unity may develop along lines which seem impossible today. There are several possible approaches which, as often happens in history, could converge at a given time, or follow closely on each other. Perhaps institutions will arise out of the need for a European deterrent force, or perhaps direct elections to the European Parliament could have an effect out of all proportion to what would, after all, only be a change in procedure. Or perhaps one day widespread demands for a European constituent assembly will come from the peoples of Western Europe themselves. The important thing will be not to miss the opportunity when it arises.

BRITAIN AND THE EUROPEAN COMMUNITY

JOHN CALMANN

OBSTACLES TO ENTRY

PRIME MINISTER HAROLD WILSON's aim of getting Britain into the European Community, stated in a number of cautious speeches in November 1966, drew little positive response from the Continent. The five Common Market countries supposedly favourable to British entry (i.e. all members except France) merely noted the statements, and the Common Market Commission gave its guarded approval. The French reaction was particularly cool, and showed no change from the position taken by Prime Minister Georges Pompidou in London in July of the same year. It was clear that France still found difficulty in accepting Britain as a real partner in Europe. The old arguments about Britain 'not being ready for the Treaty of Rome' were gone through again, even though this time they no longer carried the conviction that they once did.

For it now seems clear that both major British political parties have committed themselves to entering the European Community. Their reasons for accepting the aims of the Community after so much hesitation are varied, but basic to both the Conservative and the Labour approaches (the Liberals have always been in favour of entry) is the understanding that the Common Market represents a new force on the continent of Europe to which Britain cannot apparently provide a more attractive alternative—a force which will change, and to some extent already has changed, relationships between the members, for the Community provides a formal and institutional recognition of the interdependence of European states. Britain's difficulty in accepting such a systematic approach to relations with its neighbours has been due to the memory of a vast empire and great influence outside Europe, a memory that maintained the illusion of self-sufficiency. As will be seen, a majority in both major British parties has gradually come to recognise that self-sufficiency is no longer possible, and that whatever the cost of entering may be, the cost of staying out of the Community will probably be higher.

It is impossible, of course, to draw up a realistic balance sheet of the advantages and disadvantages of Britain's joining the Community. What seems likely is that some industries in which Britain is fairly strong, such as chemicals and fibres, mechanical engineering and automobiles, electronics and computers, and nuclear energy, would profit from the enormously expanded market provided by the Community. On the other hand, while the standard of living of Britain's farmers might improve through the

64

Common Agricultural Policy, Britain's cost of living might gradually rise as a result of an increase in the cost of food—according to some estimates the rise might be between 3 and 4 per cent. The effect on Britain's balance of payments might also be considerable, in that the Common Agricultural Policy requires countries which import food from outside the Community to pay levies on such imports into a common fund to be used for various purposes within it. If Britain joined several other countries would join as well; this could lead to modifications both in the levy system itself and in the level of payments expected from each member country. It is also possible that once Britain had joined the Community the basic methods of the Common Agricultural Policy might be changed, if it were found that it was seriously detrimental to the economy of any of the member countries.

One of the advantages of the Treaty is that it leaves the political future of the Community vague. It indicates that political union in some form is desirable, but the Six have not yet progressed very far here. Far from this uncertainty being a disadvantage for Britain, as some British critics of the Community have suggested, it provides a formidable opportunity for British statesmen to contribute something of their own to the development of the Community, for it is in the field of political institutions that Britain is most respected and admired in Europe. Political possibilities may be of even greater significance in the long run, perhaps, than the advantage of a wider market and of a planned international economy.

France's reluctance to accept Britain's desire for membership of the Community as genuine derives more from its own uncertainties about Britain than from Britain's uncertainties about the nature of the Community and what it will lead to. France's views are today very different from those of its partners on this question.

At the same time, while the other five member countries believe that British membership of the Community is desirable, they are not prepared to risk anything for it, at least not as long as there is no positive sign that Britain is really committed to entry. After the break-down of the negotiations with Britain in January 1963 it emerged that the Five were not prepared to risk a split inside the Community with France while Britain itself was divided on the issue. Their attitude would become more positive if Britain took some new initiative of its own towards Europe. As will be seen later, however, one of the main difficulties in the British approach to the problem of entry is that most of those concerned with it are hypnotised by France's opposition. In so far as this opposition is real their position is understandable; it is, however, unproductive of change, and has led to an atmosphere of deadlock, in spite of Wilson's attempts to restart negotiations.

Many reasons have been given for French intransigence, and especially that of President de Gaulle, who has paradoxically enough also shown the keenest desire to collaborate with Britain in one limited field, the aircraft industry. Since this industry is one where the British are in a stronger position than the French, in that the British industry is larger and technically more varied, the President's willingness or unwillingness to work with Britain is clearly not dictated by fear of British power and resources. On the contrary, in the summer of 1966 Pompidou seemed to be saying that Britain's current economic weaknesses meant that the country would have to wait until they had passed before it could apply for membership of the Community. One of the strongest reasons Britain has for joining, however, is the feeling that some of these difficulties would be overcome through membership. The 'cold blasts', 'axes' and 'squeezes' applied by the Labour government, meant to 'shake up' the British economy, might be obtained through the strong competition offered from the Continent, if Britain were in the Community. Above all Britain needs help with its balance of payments difficulties; to cure these it needs the continued support of its European partners. But it is precisely this support which France is reluctant to offer, for what seem to be political reasons.

Britain finds itself therefore in a deadlock with France. This is a situation which the French sometimes appear ready to exploit, thereby casting doubt on the validity of their reasons for keeping Britain out and refusing to admit the possibility of renewed negotiations. Apparently France under de Gaulle still seeks a form of national independence in which few other Western European states believe today. Military strength is still, according to some French theorists, the ultimate source of power, and economic strength important mainly in that it is needed for military strength. Thus France sets aside a large proportion (about half) of its military expenditure on the *force de frappe*—its atomic weapons system—and accuses Britain of being subservient to the United States. France regards the European Community as a method of reinforcing its economy, but does not consider that membership binds it to accept all the implications of the Treaty of Rome, such as a directly elected European parliament, common funds centrally administered, or even a common trade policy towards countries outside the Community. In other words the Community is a mechanism, in the Gaullist view, to help each member-nation survive; it is not an end in itself. Britain is a European nation with which France must remain a friendly rival; Britain's weaknesses are useful to France, therefore there is no reason to help Britain overcome them. And while a serious economic crisis in Britain, reflected in mass unemployment or a large decline in imports, is something which would possibly harm France too, a series of economic difficulties which merely hamstring its government need cause the French government little or no concern.

THE NEGOTIATIONS 1961–3: THREE MAIN PROBLEMS

France's attitude to British entry was not always as adamant; during the long negotiations from the autumn of 1961 until January 1963, France appeared, at first at any rate, to be willing to consider British membership. This is not the place to discuss the failure of these negotiations, except in so far as they revealed certain basic problems which for a long time afterwards dominated British attitudes to the Community. The seemingly interminable discussions surrounding the problems of British agriculture and of Commonwealth trade held up the negotiations for about nine months (March–December 1962), and there can be no doubt that the effect of this was not merely to disillusion the British, but also to make the French, the principal protagonists on the other side, suspect that Britain did not want to accept the Community's rules. As many writers on this subject have pointed out, these rules were made very much with French agriculture in mind.

Britain's support system and tradition of importing from cheap Commonwealth producers (who, according to the French and the Common Market Commission, are subsidised also) was changed from being a technical stumbling block into becoming a major political issue on which the British government was apparently prepared to see the negotiations stand or fall. This was probably a tactical error, for it gave de Gaulle a good opportunity to consider the probable effect of membership on the balance of forces in the

Community (and in Europe generally) much more carefully. Britain's acceptance from America of the Polaris submarine and missile system at Nassau in December 1962, a meeting from which France was excluded, confirmed him in the view that Britain could not become his partner. In Britain, however, the view persisted for some time after the French veto of 14 January 1963 on Britain's entry into the Community that agriculture and Commonwealth trade were fundamental issues, and to these two was added, particularly in the mind of the Labour Party, the question of the other countries of the European Free Trade Association (EFTA) and Britain's commitment to see that an arrangement was made between them and the Community also.

Agriculture

The insistence, however, with which the British government originally spoke of safeguards for these 'essential interests', which were required before Britain could enter the Community, was probably unnecessary. The Community's objective must obviously be to protect the essential interests of the member countries; it is the Commission's business to discover what these are, and, if necessary, to try to reorientate government thinking about them in new directions. The problems of British entry, in any case, can be said to fall, like most of those with which the Commission has to deal, into 'technical' and 'political' categories. The 'technical' are those on which the governments have committed themselves to find a solution; the 'political' imply that governments have not yet been convinced of the necessity to act, and are using talks and negotiations as a method of protecting special interests, inside their own countries. Under this definition the agricultural problem, for instance, is largely a 'technical' one, and if Britain has the 'political' will to be a member of the European Community an adequate solution to it could certainly be found. In other words, if the introduction of the Community's Common Agricultural Policy into Britain were regarded as part of the business which Britain would have to accomplish after signing the Treaty of Rome, instead of making accession to the Treaty dependent on settling agriculture first, Britain would probably find that its influence on how that policy was developed would be much greater.

The fact is that the Treaty of Rome is not regarded by most member countries as a trade arrangement but as the foundation of a new system of international relations between Western European states; the aim is to encourage both the economic development of members and their political cooperation. The effects of the Common Agricultural Policy of the Community may not be entirely to Britain's liking, especially where the question of balance of payments is concerned, but until Britain joins it is almost impossible to know exactly what the effect on the country would be, or what adjustments would have to be made to solve its special problems. It has been suggested by some agriculturists that British horticulture, poultry and dairy farming might all be adversely affected by the application of the Common Agricultural Policy; given a transition period (discussed below) and a reconsideration of problems such as these by a Commission in which British interests would be heard, it can be expected with some confidence that changes in the present structure of farming in Britain would be carried out sufficiently gradually to cushion farmers against adverse effects. In the latter half of 1966, indeed, the attitude of the British government to this question seemed to change so that agriculture is now talked of more as a problem which will have to be faced than as an insuperable obstacle to entry.

The Commonwealth

The Commonwealth problem has also changed since the time of the negotiations. It was then feared that the Community would continue to give preferences to the ex-French (and ex-Belgian) colonies in Africa, while the ex-British colonies and territories, which comprised much larger areas, much greater populations and a much wider variety of economies, would be neglected. It was the British government's aim that the 'white' Commonwealth should also find at least as great an outlet for its traditional exports as these countries (Australia, New Zealand and Canada) had found in Britain; at the same time the developing Commonwealth countries like India or Nigeria would obviously have to benefit from the Community's aid programmes. At the time it also seemed that some countries, like Nigeria, would simply shun the Community, and leave the Commonwealth if Britain entered it, because they regarded it as a 'neo-colonialist' enterprise.

All this was reversed soon after the negotiations collapsed. India, Nigeria and the countries of East Africa as well as the 'white' Commonwealth established their own direct relations with the Community and many have sought to obtain some form of trade or aid agreement with it. Such an agreement between Nigeria and the Community, held up by France's six-month-long defection from the Council of Ministers in 1965, came into force in 1966; the East African countries are still negotiating theirs. Canada, Australia and New Zealand have permanent representatives in Brussels, but no formal negotiations are yet in progress. Their exports will, however, be considered in the framework of the 'Kennedy Round' of trade negotiations in GATT which are still going on. The concessions made to India, Pakistan and Ceylon by the Community during the negotiations with Britain have in part at least been put into practice since; for instance, tea enters the Community free of duty or quota restrictions. The 'white' Commonwealth countries are also being encouraged by Britain to seek new markets, as Britain cannot by itself continue to provide a tied outlet for their exports while they protect their own industries with tariffs against British products. New Zealand seems to be the only one of these countries which is still heavily dependent on the British market for its lamb and butter.

Today the problem of the Commonwealth is in many ways more political than economic. Indeed, while the question of Commonwealth trade has turned out to be less important than it seemed in 1962, the question of Western Europe's relations with the rest of the world, developing or developed, has become more urgent; as the transformation of the old imperial relationship is completed, and as Britain gradually reduces its commitments in the Far East, it will be increasingly necessary for Europeans to look at the rest of the world as a whole, and not in terms of their own former relationships with various parts of it. The Community will no longer find it so easy to restrict its aid to France's ex-colonies or those of Belgium and the Netherlands, and will be under great pressure to consider providing outlets for goods from Latin America and Asia as well as Africa. Several Mediterranean countries (Morocco, Algeria, Tunisia, Israel and Yugoslavia) are engaged on negotiations with the Community already; Greece and Turkey have become associate members. Developed countries like Canada and Australia on the other hand will have to get more accustomed to establishing their own relationship with the countries that are nearer to them, especially in the Pacific, instead of assuming that their foreign policies can be managed from London or Washington or conducted on the basis of sentimental attachments to the mother country. Developed or not, all these countries seek help, material, technical and educational, from Europe (as well as hoping to sell there), and it is obviously going to be easier to answer this need if Europeans act in concert and pool their resources for aid, than if each country competes with its neighbours in trying to conserve its former sphere of influence.

This is a long-term political problem, which can probably be most usefully discussed after Britain has joined the Community; certainly the economic problems involved in Commonwealth trade, like those of agriculture, can be regarded as 'technical' and need not be obstacles to British entry any more. On the other hand the political problems involved are not likely to decrease with time, and far from dampening British enthusiasm for the Community the need for a common approach to the rest of the world should encourage Britain to seek membership. This, of course, involves the other EFTA countries as well.

EFTA

The British commitment to the EFTA countries took the form of promising them that Britain would not leave the organisation without finding some acceptable arrangements with the Six for all the members who wished to have them. This commitment was considered particularly important by the Labour opposition in Britain during the negotiations for entry into the Community; they felt it was a legitimate reason for withholding their support for the government's position in Brussels. Since the Labour Party has taken office, however, one EFTA country, Austria, has begun negotiations on its own with the Community, which may lead to its becoming an associate member and thus to its withdrawal from EFTA. The Danes have been held back by their loyalty to the British, and this is also true of the Norwegians; in the autumn of 1966, however, the Danish government began to show interest in making a separate approach. Portugal as a developing country is a special case, and will require special treatment should it wish to join the Community; Sweden and Switzerland remain, and it is unlikely that Britain would allow its entry into the Community to be held up by the neutralist qualms of these two countries.

The difficulty that the entry of the EFTA countries represents for the European Community is that it would add enormously to the heavy load of technical and administrative problems which the Commission has to bear. It would probably be hard for all the countries to join simultaneously, or to conduct their negotiations with the Community at once. The amount of special cases and special treatments each is likely to wish to discuss is considerable, and so a carefully organised timetable would have to be prepared in order to fit their membership in with Britain's. The pressure on the Commission would increase enormously, and it is possible that it would be forced to seek new powers, and greater scope to reach decisions quickly. This is all calculated to deter the French government, which sees no need to hurry the process of patching up the division of Europe represented by the existence of EFTA and the EEC, and which would not wish for any increase in the powers of the Commission which an extension of the Community's area might bring with it. Thus the main political difficulties associated with the entry of the EFTA countries into the Community (apart from the question of Switzerland's and Sweden's neutrality, which concerns them alone) come from French fears of what will happen to the Community; it is possible, however, that French attitudes to the progress of European integration will change under the pressure of circumstances. From the point of view of the

EFTA countries themselves the problems are technical, and membership of the Community is a question of time. It can be said, therefore, with some certainty that if Britain joined the Community, arrangements for dealing with the other EFTA countries would follow automatically, and would not provide an obstacle to British membership.

A Transition Period?

Thus the three great stumbling-blocks of the 1961–3 negotiations have been transformed, both in themselves and in the way the British government, manned by a party originally hostile to the Community, looks at them. These problems will be the stuff of future talks, but it is unlikely that they could hold them up once they had begun. The adjustment to Community methods and policies would have to be made gradually; that is to say not during the negotiations themselves, but during a 'transition period', in which Britain would be a member of the Community, take part in the discussions of the Council of Ministers and contribute to the development of the common policies. In this period Britain could also adapt its agricultural system to fit in with that of the Community, seek to establish the basis of a new relationship with the Commonwealth countries and bring in its EFTA partners as well as introduce the many tariff and tax (and other) changes which the Six have already effected within the Community.

All this would require a large number of administrative changes, and could therefore not be done overnight. The length of such a transition period would be a major item of the negotiations; it would probably have to be fairly long, possibly five years or more. If there were no time-limit, or if a longer limit were set, the application of the Community's system might be spun out indefinitely by governments unwilling to sacrifice support from voters who might for a short while be adversely affected by the changes. The supporters of British entry both on the Continent and in Britain have frequently said in the last few years that the next round of negotiations should be short and successful: by allowing for a transition period this would become much easier to achieve administratively speaking.

The commitment by all major parties to seek British membership is to some extent a reflection of the fundamental recognition by the British public that the country can no longer survive on its own, that the British need their neighbours, just as in the long run their neighbours need them. The Conservative Party has repeatedly declared its commitment to getting Britain 'into Europe', but its influence in opposition is largely a propagandist one, and it cannot decide policy. There also seems to be a tendency among Tories to seek arrangements with General de Gaulle, as if British membership depended only on him; there is no interest in finding closer ties with West Germany. This attitude is also present in the Labour government's policy, which rests on French objections and apparently sees no alternative to wooing or threatening France. At the same time the Labour Party, since coming into office, has moved significantly closer to accepting the Treaty of Rome, and in November 1966 the government made it clear that membership of the Community is the principal aim of British policy in Europe.

Getting Support For Britain

The difficulty is going to be to convince all concerned of British sincerity, especially France under de Gaulle. It is widely felt among advocates of

British entry that the first aim ought to be to get active support for British membership from among the Five, who have not so far shown themselves willing to take any risks on Britain's behalf. For them to become so willing, the British government must give a clear indication that its commitment to Europe comes first. A new approach from Britain is the answer to this problem, not a passive acceptance of the status quo accompanied by complaints of French intransigence, which has been the basis of the discussion in Britain so far.

The history of British relations with the Six since the war can be said to fall roughly into three stages. First, until the end of the 1950s Britain remained suspicious and even hostile to all proposals to integrate the economies, the defence, or the political structure of Western Europe, and stuck to the 'three-circle' theory, of each of which Britain was a member: the Commonwealth, the Atlantic world and the United States, and Europe. The second stage came when Prime Minister Harold Macmillan became aware that Britain was going to be excluded from an important economic development in the shape of the Common Market, and proposed that the Six should join with Britain and other European countries in a Free Trade Area; this was rejected by the Six as being too loose a structure. The third development was the commitment to Europe which the Conservative government made in 1961 when it opened the negotiations to join the Common Market. This commitment was hidden from the public, because Macmillan feared the consequences for his party if his hand was too openly revealed; it is also possible that neither he nor his ministers, including Edward Heath, were fully aware of the political implications of starting these negotiations.

In effect the negotiations began a process of education in Britain, through which all the major political groups attached to both main parties found they had to take the development of the Community seriously. Instead of the Rome Treaty being, as Labour Leader Hugh Gaitskell seemed to think it was, a trade arrangement which aimed to hamstring governments and prevent socialist policies, it was clearly the basis of a major political institution, which in due course became important enough even for General de Gaulle to attack it. In 1965-6 it became increasingly clear that the development of such a political institution is something which has captured the imaginations not only of the British civil service, and the Foreign Office in particular, but of some members of the government. But as we have seen, Britain is apparently still faced by the stone wall of France's objections.

This is because Britain has not yet reached the fourth stage of attempting an initiative itself towards Europe, one which does not merely pose the problem of British commitment to the Community, but which offers the Six something new. One reason for this is that the 1966 Labour government is still a recent if not reluctant convert to the idea of close ties with Europe, and apparently still fears anything which would diminish what the Prime Minister refers to as 'our sovereignty'. Leaving aside the philosophical vagueness of this term, the practical implications are that the government is reluctant to commit itself as yet to a European policy which might yield some results. One advantage for the Prime Minister in taking over the Conservative position on the Common Market is that it has no immediate consequences. In fact, new ideas which could come from Britain about a possible European technological union and a new common defence organisation to replace NATO, on both of which Britain has plenty to offer its neighbours, are mentioned only in passing, or kept in files far from the light of day.

NEW BRITISH INITIATIVES

Technological union

Such ideas have, however, been mooted for some time now by active 'Europeans' in Britain and by those concerned with preparing policy in Whitehall. It is impossible here to give more than a rough sketch of what they involve but it is worthwhile to mention them even if only very shortly, because in 1967–8 it is possible that the transformation of Britain's relations with the rest of Western Europe will involve a radical new departure. By 'technological union' is meant an organisation which would attempt to pool the resources of its member countries in a number of advanced technological industries. These include air transport, computers, nuclear energy and space, all of which are fields in which European countries have already begun to work, but in which Britain still has a lead in Europe. In Britain these industries employ more people than in any other European country, and most important of all, the extent of the research and development effort in Britain in these fields is larger also. What Britain lacks at present is the ability to increase this effort, mainly because the cost of doing so is greatly beyond the resources of a country of Britain's size, and also because the country lacks the qualified manpower. Britain is trying to cooperate to some extent with France in the aircraft industry (where it has too much manpower), but the aim of a technological union would be to go well beyond the limits of bilateral cooperation in one industry. The aim would be to help those countries, which, like Germany, have access to capital but have little or no research and development effort and limited technological resources. Indeed it is in the technological field that Britain would probably find Germany most interested in becoming its partner.

The way such a technological union might work is for the member countries to set up a joint institution, which would be given funds for research and for aid to investment in the industries concerned; these funds would be fixed for a defined period, probably about five years. The institution would have powers to direct research into fields which it felt were particularly important and to make sure that the results of such work were published or made available to interested parties in the member countries; this would avoid the duplication of effort which the existence of several national programmes in Europe makes inevitable today. Britain's particular contribution could be to provide scientists and engineers for joint research schemes. The institution would also have funds to use for investment in the industries concerned, much as the High Authority of the ECSC has been able to help the modernisation of the coal and steel industries of the Community with special investment aid. The introduction of automated methods of production, frequently feared by both management and labour for its possibly disruptive effects, might be furthered by programmes financed by this common institution and aimed at training people in new methods and especially in the use of computers, and at helping workers who became redundant through the introduction of labour-saving systems. (This particular aspect of modernisation has been very successfully dealt with in the ECSC through the High Authority's 'readaptation schemes' which have helped about 200,000 redundant coal-miners in the Six. A technological union would probably not have to deal with such large numbers, but the methods used in coalmining could probably be applied in other industries also).

If Britain were anxious to discuss such a plan with Germany it might find a much more lively and positive response than for its perennial attempts to get the Germans to cover the currency loss involved in British expenditure on troops in Germany by buying British equipment. The Germans have pointed out time and time again that they are not interested in buying things they do not need, just in order to help with balance of payments problems. A much more sensible approach would be to find out what the Germans do need, and then to seek to make arrangements with them which would have attractions for both sides. For Britain there would be not only the advantage of more amiable and productive cooperation with Germany in the advanced technological industries, in which Germany's needs are great (and its dependence on the United States burdensome) but also the political asset that Britain would at last find an active partner in Europe. Other countries would of course be encouraged to join, and it is likely that Italy, Benelux and the Scandinavian countries would also be interested; and France could not long remain on its own.

An approach on defence

On the defence side, Britain is at present engaged on talks with Germany and the United States on the question of reducing the number of troops stationed in Germany—though the reasons for this are more to do with balance of payments than with strategy. (It also seems to be the belief of the United States government that this is a way of reaching new agreements with the Soviet Union.) France has withdrawn from active support of NATO though still committed under Article 5 of the NATO treaty to come to the defence of its allies in the event of their being attacked. The unreality of the present NATO system, with its heavy dependence on the American nuclear deterrent, its lack of a joint procurement system, its separate but individually ineffective national forces (as far as the European members are concerned) and its lack of a common concept of present-day strategic needs, is beginning to make itself felt in Europe; lip-service is paid to the NATO idea, but each country is beginning to seek a new understanding with Eastern Europe on its own, and the outlook for joint procurement of weapons has never been so bleak.

If Britain were to seek to create a new European defence system, based on close cooperation with Germany and allied to the United States (something which the Americans themselves seem to be advocating now) but on the basis of a new treaty, it is possible that the idea would gain considerable political support on the Continent. The object of the treaty would be to try to create a common European approach to defence problems, without France, if need be, in the initial stages. (The mistake being made currently in the Conservative Party is to suppose that a pooling of French and British nuclear forces would have the same psychological effect; the French are simply not interested in such an idea, and the rest of Europe, and especially the Germans, would regard it as an attempt by the two countries least committed to European integration to dominate the rest. The government, by comparison, remains entirely preoccupied with NATO on the one hand, and attempting to get 'off-set' payments from Germany on the other, and disregards the need for a 'European' approach to defence altogether.)

COMMITMENT WITHOUT A POLICY

In both these fields, advanced technology and defence, Britain still seems determined to 'go it alone'. In the aircraft industry, it is true, Britain is cooperating with France, but both countries are doing this with glances over their shoulders to see what chances there are of surviving on their own. This industry is too limited, and the market available probably too small for this form of cooperation to be much more than an administrative experiment. In defence the government is still not certain whether Europe is its main commitment or whether Britain needs to be involved in the Far East, and is still deeply concerned with a 'special relationship' with the United States, whose existence is, however, hard to prove. The main difficulty Britain has in getting into the Community, if such is its aim, is to get enough political support from the Five to make France feel that it will be out on a limb if a veto on British entry is attempted a second time. This support can be obtained only by positive measures, initiatives such as those described above, which would prove that Britain is now prepared to merge its future completely with that of its neighbours in the Community.

In January 1967 it was clear that French policy was aimed at holding up British entry for as long as possible. Direct refusal to consider the question had so far been ruled out, partly because General de Gaulle was afraid of the effects such a move would have on the French parliamentary elections, and partly because the French government was becoming more aware of the limitations of nationalistic policies in Europe and their isolating effects. The possibility of spinning out the preliminary talks, by introducing irrelevancies such as the price of gold, remained open to him, however, with the result that this preliminary phase appeared likely to take a long time. It was, of course, possible that Wilson and Brown, in their diplomatic assault on the Six in January and February 1967, would persuade the five countries favourable to British entry to seek to force France to accept the new member, if necessary with threats to leave France on its own. This, however, was an unlikely development. In any event Wilson's commitment to entering the Common Market, however ambiguously it has sometimes been expressed, and whatever the motives for it may originally have been, has had the effect of strengthening the position of the institutions of the European Community and their supporters in the Six, and means that the aims of some of their critics, such as General de Gaulle, who wish seriously to modify their influence on member governments and nations, are going to be more difficult to realise. Thus, in spite of his former doubts about its value Wilson's approach to the European Community has made a real contribution to its vitality and this in itself will perhaps ensure that Britain will become a member, however long it takes.

For Further Reading

OFFICIAL DOCUMENTS:

Treaty establishing the ECSC (Paris Treaty): English edition published by the High Authority of the ECSC, Luxembourg, 1952.

Treaty establishing the EEC (Rome Treaty): English edition published by the Commission of the EEC, Brussels, 1958 (there is also an English edition published by HMSO, London).

Treaty establishing Euratom (Euratom Treaty): English edition published by Euratom Commission, Brussels, 1958.

Rapport au Parlement Européen sur l'Etat des négociations avec le Royaume-Uni, EEC Commission, Brussels, 1963 (English translation available).

PERIODICALS:

The Economist, London, 14 May 1966: special issue entitled *Europe in a Shrinking World*.

European Community (monthly), European Communities Information Service, London.

Journal of Common Market Studies (quarterly), Basil Blackwell, Oxford. In particular III, 3, July 1965: 'The Future of Britain's Relations with Europe'.

Opera Mundi-Europe (weekly report on the economy of the Common Market), English ed. European Intelligence Ltd, Tunbridge Wells.

BOOKS:

Beever, R. Colin. *European Unity and the Trade Union Movement*, Sijthoff, Leyden; Gregory Lounz, New York, 1960.

Beloff, Nora. *The General Says No: Britain's Exclusion from Europe*, Penguin, London, 1963; Peter Smith, Gloucester, Mass.

Campbell, Alan and Thompson, Denis. *Common Market Law: Texts and Commentaries*, Stevens, London; Rothmans, South Hackensuck, NJ, 1962.

Camps, Miriam. *Britain and the European Community 1955–1963*, Oxford Univ. Press, London and New York, 1964. *What Kind of Europe?* Chatham House Essays No. 8, Oxford Univ. Press for Royal Institute of International Affairs, London and New York, 1965.

Deniau, Jean F. *The Common Market*, Barrie and Rockliff/Pall Mall Press, London; Frederick A. Praeger, New York, 3rd ed. 1965.

Forsyth, Murray. *The Parliament of the European Communities*, Political and Economic Planning, London, 1964.

Hallstein, Walter. *United Europe: Challenge and Opportunity*, Oxford Univ. Press, London; Harvard Univ. Press, Cambridge, Mass., 1962.

Lindberg, Leon N. *The Political Dynamics of European Economic Integration*, Oxford Univ. Press, London; Stanford Univ. Press, Stanford, Calif., 1963.

Lippmann, Walter. *Western Unity and the Common Market*, Hamish Hamilton, London; Little, Brown, Boston, Mass., 1962.

Tracy, Michael. *Agriculture in Western Europe*, Jonathan Cape, London; Frederick A. Praeger, New York, 1964.

Uri, Pierre. *Partnership for Progress: A Program for Transatlantic Action*, Harper and Row for Atlantic Institute, New York and London, 1963.

75

Notes on Contributors

BURGESS, TONY. Read economics at London University. After working in advertising turned to economic journalism in 1957, writing for *Petroleum Press Service*, *Euromarket* and *Business*. Appointed to staff of European Communities Information Service in Luxembourg, 1962 as editor of the Service's English-language publications. Press Officer in the Information Service's London office, 1964–6.

CALMANN, JOHN. Born in Hamburg, emigrated with his family to England in 1937. After leaving Oxford University, where he read history, he worked for the *Wall Street Journal* in New York and then for the European Community in Luxembourg, where he was first in the publications department of the Information Service and then a spokesman for the High Authority of the ECSC. He then became editor of the English edition of *Opera Mundi-Europe*, and later carried out a study of the political aspects of European cooperation in defence technology for the Institute for Strategic Studies, London. Currently employed by a publishing house in London.

PRAG, DEREK. Read modern languages and economics at Cambridge University; studied Slavonic languages at Cambridge and London. Journalist at Reuters, London, Brussels and Madrid; head of English-language Section, ECSC information service, 1955–9; head of Publications Division, European Communities Information Service, Brussels/Luxembourg, 1959–65; head of European Communities Information Service, London from 1966.

PRYCE, ROY, Ph.D.(Cantab.). Fellow of Emmanuel College, Cambridge, 1955–7; Fellow of St Antony's College, Oxford, 1955–7. Head of the London Office, European Communities Information Service, 1957–64; Rockefeller Research Fellow, 1964–5. Currently Lecturer in Politics and Director of Contemporary European Studies, University of Sussex.

URI, PIERRE. Studied at the École Normale Supérieure, the Faculté de Droit of the Sorbonne and Princeton University. Economic and Financial Councillor to the Commissariat Général du Plan, 1947–52; member of United Nations Committee of Experts on Full Employment, 1949; Economic Director of the ECSC, 1952–9; chairman of Experts Group on the Long-term Development of the EEC, 1960–4; now Economic Consultant to the Atlantic Institute near Paris. Publications include *La crise de la zone de libre-échange*, 1959; *Dialogue des continents*, 1963; and reports on the Schuman Plan, 1951 and on the economic situation of the EEC, 1958.

Index

An essential work of reference

WESTERN EUROPE: A HANDBOOK

Edited by John Calmann

This book is the third in the series *Handbooks to the Modern World*. It cover
the political, economic, social and cultural facts and concerns of Wester
Europe today—an area stretching from Iceland to Turkey which ha
emerged as a separate unit only within the last generation.

Part One provides detailed basic information, with maps and statistics
about each Western European country (geography and population, con
stitutional system, recent history, economy, social security, the press, etc.)
A number of distinguished authorities contribute to Parts Two and Three
Part Two consists of essays on important questions affecting all or most o
Western Europe, and case studies of individual countries. Part Thre
contains a guide to the structure of the European Community and the othe
cooperative organisations, and essays on European integration as so fa
experienced.

The Paris and Rome Treaties which established the European Communit
represent a revolutionary challenge to the traditional concept of the nation
state. A common system of institutions within which national administration
work together instead of competing is a new idea in world history and i
being realised in Western Europe now. In this book individual countries ar
treated as far as possible in joint perspective, their common problems bein
emphasised rather than their national characteristics.

For those concerned in industry, economics, education, journalism
politics and diplomacy *Western Europe: A Handbook* is essential as an autho
ritative and comprehensive work of reference.

736 pages; 20 pages of maps; half-tone illustrations; bibliographies; index

£7 7s. net
in U.K. only